CAN YOU CRACK THE CODE?

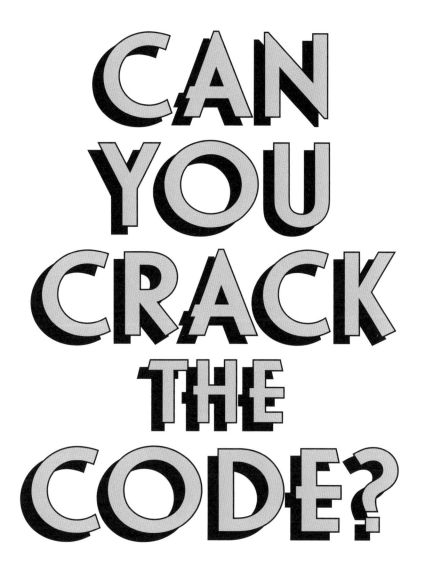

CAN YOU CRACK THE CODE?

A FASCINATING HISTORY OF CIPHERS AND CRYPTOGRAPHY

ELLA SCHWARTZ

illustrated by **LILY WILLIAMS**

BLOOMSBURY
CHILDREN'S BOOKS

NEW YORK LONDON OXFORD NEW DELHI SYDNEY

BLOOMSBURY CHILDREN'S BOOKS
Bloomsbury Publishing Inc., part of Bloomsbury Publishing Plc
1385 Broadway, New York, NY 10018

BLOOMSBURY, BLOOMSBURY CHILDREN'S BOOKS, and the Diana logo
are trademarks of Bloomsbury Publishing Plc

First published in the United States of America in March 2019
by Bloomsbury Children's Books

Bloomsbury books may be purchased for business or promotional use. For information on bulk purchases please contact
Macmillan Corporate and Premium Sales Department at specialmarkets@macmillan.com

Library of Congress Cataloging-in-Publication Data
Names: Schwartz, Ella, author.
Title: Can you crack the code? / by Ella Schwartz.
Description: New York : Bloomsbury, [2019]
Identifiers: LCCN 2018011662 (print) • LCCN 2018020549 (e-book)
ISBN 978-1-68119-514-8 (hardcover) • ISBN 978-1-68119-989-4 (e-book)
Subjects: LCSH: Ciphers—Juvenile literature. | Ciphers—History—Juvenile literature. |
Cryptography—Juvenile literature. | Cryptography—History—Juvenile literature.
Classification: LCC Z103.3 .S378 2019 (print) | LCC Z103.3 (e-book) | DDC 652/.8—dc23
LC record available at https://lccn.loc.gov/2018011662

Book design by Danielle Ceccolini
Typeset by Westchester Publishing Services
Printed in China by C & C Offset Printing Co., Ltd. Shenzhen, Guangdong
2 4 6 8 10 9 7 5 3 1

All papers used by Bloomsbury Publishing Plc are natural, recyclable products made from wood grown in well-managed
forests. The manufacturing processes conform to the environmental regulations of the country of origin.

To find out more about our authors and books visit www.bloomsbury.com and sign up for our newsletters.

For Jeff, who cracked the code to my heart

CAN YOU CRACK THE CODE?

CONTENTS

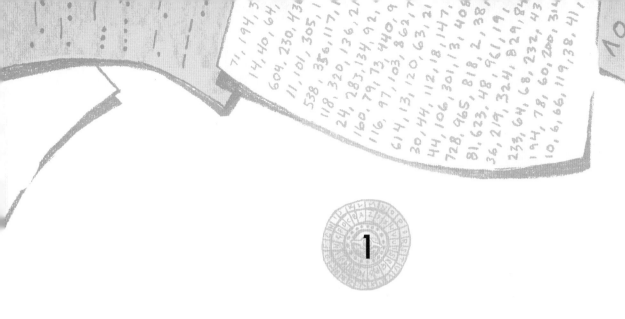

1

CAN YOU CRACK THE CODE?

There are codes all around you, designed to keep secrets safe or keep you out of places you don't belong. Some codes are designed to keep a computer system safe from hackers. Other codes are designed to keep secrets safe from prying eyes.

Can you crack the code?

When we talk about cracking the code, what do we really mean? Breaking into something? Discovering a hidden message? Hacking into something you probably were never supposed to see?

Yes to all that!

Cracking the code means revealing a secret.

A secret is only a secret as long as it doesn't fall into the wrong hands. The minute a secret is exposed, it stops being a secret. Then it's just information—information that was never meant to be revealed. There are many reasons someone may not want to reveal this information. It could spoil a special surprise, it might be embarrassing, or it could be very damaging.

Whatever the reason for having a secret, the goal is: keep the secret safe!

So, can you crack the code? Can you uncover the secret? The codemaker sure hopes not. They've gone to a lot of trouble to keep the secret safe.

This begins the battle between codemakers and codebreakers. Since ancient history, codemakers have worked very hard to build the strongest codes to protect their most important secrets, but codebreakers keep finding more powerful methods for cracking those codes. As the codemakers get more sophisticated, so do the codebreakers.

This book will teach you all about cryptography, encryption, hacking, and cyber-security. All of that is pretty cool, but there's more! This book is more than meets the eye. It's not just a book. It's actually one big secret for you to crack. Read it carefully. Only the smartest codebreakers will spot all the clues in this book to crack the code and unlock the secret.

Will you crack the code?

Let's find out.

2

A TALE OF CODES AND CIPHERS

Keeping Secrets Safe

Secrets are important.

Keeping a secret safe is just as important.

One way someone might choose to protect a secret is by pretending there is no secret. If someone doesn't suspect you have a secret they are not going to go snooping. This is the idea behind the ancient practice of **steganography**. Steganography is a type of communication where a message is kept hidden. The word "steganography" comes from two Greek words: *steganos*, which means "covered," and *graphein*, which means "to write." Covered writing. In other words, hidden secrets.

Steganography has been used throughout history. When the ancient Chinese wanted to send a secret message, they wrote the message on silk, scrunched the silk into a tight ball, then covered the ball in wax. The messenger would then swallow the ball of wax. To deliver the message, you can imagine what the messenger had to do next—yuck.

The ancient Greeks also used steganography to keep their

messages hidden. One technique they used was shaving a messenger's head, tattooing a message on his scalp, and waiting for the hair to grow back before sending the messenger to the destination. Obviously, the message couldn't have been all that urgent!

Steganography is even used today by secret agents around the world. The tool? Invisible ink. A secret agent uses a special kind of ink to write a message. When the ink dries, it becomes invisible. The recipient would need to know that to reveal the hidden words, they would have to heat the ink until the message reappears.

Secret agents can also hide a message in what, at first glance, may appear like a boring note. But if the recipient knows what to look for, a secret might be revealed. Take a look at the sentences below:

Cole rises and cooks kale. Then he eats. Cole only drinks espresso.

Simple enough? Nothing sneaky going on, right?

If the recipient of the message knows what to look for, though, they can find a secret message hidden in that text. Notice the first letters of each of the words:

Cole rises and cooks kale. Then he eats. Cole only drinks espresso.

Now put all these letters together to form the secret message:

Crack the code

This isn't the only way to use steganography to hide a secret message in plain sight. Take a look at the block of characters below:

```
CAESAR2LIKEHOPBABY59HIC
MEET4LOVEJUNGLE43APPLE7
SEVEN7FORESTANDCAR67BAT
SEND7OVER6ATMEFOR89540O
CREDIT4MATH7APRIL30HOME
LIBRARYAUGUST19ATWISH4Y
REMEMBER9TO7THINK5IN8ON
THE5ALLEYMARCH4EASY1974
```

On first glance, the text above appears like a random string of letters and numbers, but if you look carefully, you'll notice words: JUNGLE, LIBRARY, HOME, MATH, MARCH, and others. Is there a secret message hidden here? You bet there is! But how to decode it? For that you'll need a special decoder.

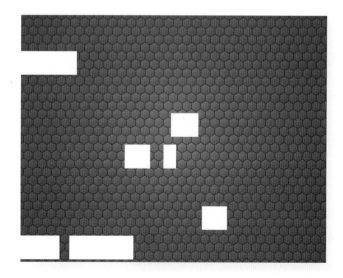

Place the decoder on top of the message, and here's what you get:

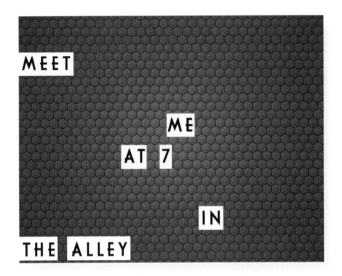

Can you see the message now?

Meet me at 7 in the alley

Today, steganography is not just about concealing a written message; the term can also be used to describe hiding digital information, usually within computer files, digital pictures, or digital music.

Hiding a secret is a great first step to preserving the secret, but steganography has one big problem. If someone intercepts the secret, the cat is out of the bag.

If a secret message is really important, not only would you want to hide the *message*, you would also want to hide the *meaning* of the message.

And that's where codes come in very handy.

In a **code**, a word or phrase is replaced with a different word to keep the original word a secret. For example, secret agents might use code names instead of their real names to prevent someone from guessing their true identity. Agent Blue might actually be a code name for a fellow named John Smith from Topeka, Kansas. John Smith probably wouldn't want his enemies knowing his true identity and knocking on his door in the middle of dinner, so a code name comes in handy—and it's pretty cool too.

Similarly, in football, a quarterback may use special code words to tell players on his team what play to make. In this case, the quarterback will call out code words that the team has memorized prior to the game, indicating the next play. "Blue 23, Blue 29 . . ."

To keep track of many code words, you may need a **codebook**, which is like a code dictionary. A codebook is a list of all the secret code words and what those codes mean. For example, an entry in a code book would look like:

John Smith = Agent Blue

Be careful not to lose the codebook! If the codebook is found, all the secrets will be revealed, then you'll need to make new code words—and that's a whole lot of work.

CODE NAME POTUS

The POTUS (or President of the United States) is protected by the Secret Service twenty-four hours a day. The Secret Service is an elite agency in charge of keeping the president and their family safe.

Long ago, to keep the presidential family secure, the Secret Service assigned code names to the president and every member of their family. When Secret Service agents discussed the whereabouts or schedule of the presidential family, only those who were supposed to have this information could understand it. This way, someone who may have been secretly listening in on a Secret Service agent's conversation would have had no idea that it was actually about the POTUS. Today, presidential code names aren't kept secret anymore. They are assigned to the presidential family more as a tradition, but also because it's often easier and quicker to recite the code name than the president's actual full name.

Here are some of the coolest POTUS code names:

Barack Obama—Renegade

Bill Clinton—Eagle

Ciphers: Not Your Everyday Code

A **cipher** is a special type of code. Some people use the words "code" and "cipher" to mean the same thing, but real codemakers and -breakers know the difference. A cipher doesn't require a codebook to figure out the secret message. Instead, a cipher requires mathematics. What? You never realized math could be sneaky? In fact, there is an entire branch of engineering called **cryptography**, which relies entirely on math to keep messages secret. The more sophisticated the mathematics, the harder a cipher is to crack.

To help understand how to convert a message into a cipher, let's meet Alice and Bob.

Alice and Bob are best friends. Like all best friends, they love to share secrets. But there's always that one eavesdropping classmate. We will call her Eve for short.

Alice wants to tell Bob an important secret. But they want to make sure the eavesdropper, Eve, doesn't discover the secret. To help understand the idea behind this secret exchange, we can imagine Alice writing down her secret, placing the secret in a box, and locking the box using a combination only known to Alice and Bob. This process can be thought of as **encryption**. When Bob receives the locked box, he opens the box with the combination. This process can be thought of as **decryption**.

Alice doesn't use an actual lock, but instead she decides to use a cipher to "lock" the message. That way, even if Eve gets her hands on the secret, she will never be able to understand it. Encryption is the process Alice uses to create the cipher for Bob. Decryption is the process Bob uses to understand the cipher.

CRYPTO CRUSADERS

In the cryptography universe, Alice and Bob are the undisputed super-heroes, saving the digital world from evil hackers. Over the years, Alice and Bob have been on many adventures together. They've evaded snoopers and saved the digital world countless times using a rare superpower: encryption.

Just who are Alice and Bob? And what's up with all the secret code talking?

Alice and Bob are not just characters used in this book. Any respectable discussion about cryptography usually tells the story of these two charac-ters. They are the official protagonists of the cryptography world.

The reason? Convenience.

Explaining cryptography can sometimes be tricky. Here's an example:

**Party A sends an encrypted message to party B
using a substitution cipher with a key of +5.**

That's a little confusing, right? A, B, 5. So many variables!

Engineers realized they needed an easier way to explain cryptog-raphy ideas. So they had the idea to replace A with Alice and B with Bob:

**Alice sends an encrypted message to Bob using
a substitution cipher.**

Much easier to understand, right?

The names Alice and Bob were chosen randomly because they start with the letters *A* and *B*. Over time, additional characters have been used to help expand the cryptography story. Carol or Charlie represent the letter *C* and are usually the third participants in an encrypted conversation. David and Dan are next to the party, representing the *D* variable.

But the letter *E*?

E is always reserved for the villain of the story: the nosy, eavesdropping Eve.

Hail Emperor Caesar

One of the earliest known ciphers was invented by the Roman emperor Julius Caesar, over two thousand years ago. It is believed that Caesar used ciphers to protect messages for his military. It was very important for Caesar to keep messages secret from his enemies because if any of his messages had been intercepted it would have destroyed all of Caesar's military plans. Secret communication was very important to Julius Caesar, and it was probably one of the reasons Caesar was so successful.

The cipher Julius Caesar invented is sometimes called a **Caesar cipher**. It is also sometimes called a **substitution cipher**, because to create the cipher, Caesar *substituted* each letter of his message with another letter. But

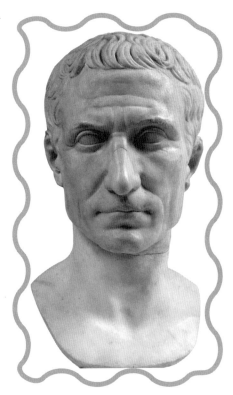

Bust of Julius Caesar

Caesar didn't substitute random letters. That would make it impossible for the recipient to decrypt. Caesar had a system to his substitution. The letter he substituted was a pre-selected number of positions farther along in the alphabet. This was called the **shift key**. For example, when a shift key of +3 was selected, every letter is shifted forward in the alphabet by three. This means that every letter *A* in the message was substituted by the letter three positions away, which is the letter *D*.

If Caesar's enemies were to get their hands on the cipher text, it would look like gibberish. They would have no idea they were in possession of military secrets.

Two thousand years ago, Julius Caesar knew that keeping secrets safe was the key to his political success. Not much has changed in two thousand years. Today, governments and militaries around the world know how important it is to keep secrets safe.

Julius Caesar is well known as one of the most successful generals in history, responsible for the rise of the Roman Empire—due in no small part to a simple cipher.

PIGSKIN PLAYBOOK

For professional football players, the top-secret codebook containing the team's secret code words is considered sacred. In some ways, the secret codebook, which can be hundreds of pages long, is considered even more important than a player's helmet or team uniform. This is because if the codebook is ever lost, the opposing team will know all the secret code words for the team's plays. Some professional football players are so paranoid about losing the codebook, they go to bed with it under their pillow! They even protect the codebook by taking it to the bathroom with them, just in case.

Punishment for losing a codebook in the National Football League can be very severe. Players can be fined up to ten thousand dollars! Worse than the hefty penalty is the severe scolding the player would get from his coach and fellow teammates.

Today, some football teams take advantage of technology and use iPads to store their codebooks rather than lugging around a heavy manual. The file is always password-protected on the iPad, just in case the device is lost or stolen.

CAMP CRYPTO

Let's pretend you're in Julius Caesar's army and you've just received this cipher message on the battlefield:

L fdph, L vdz, L frqtxhuhg!

It's up to you to decrypt the message. What are you going to do?

The first thing you need to know is the key. Without the key the message will be very hard to crack. Luckily, before you marched out to battle, Caesar told you the decryption key would be +3. Now you have everything you need to decrypt the message.

With a +3 shift key, every letter in the alphabet is shifted forward by three to create a cipher, so

A → D
B → E
C → F
D → G

And so on . . .

Letters in the original message are called **plaintext**. Letters in the encrypted message are called **cipher letters**. Here's how a plaintext alphabet would correspond to cipher letters with a shift key of +3:

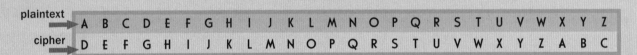

plaintext
A B C D E F G H I J K L M N O P Q R S T U V W X Y Z

cipher
D E F G H I J K L M N O P Q R S T U V W X Y Z A B C

Let's begin decrypting the cipher. The first cipher letter is *L*. The corresponding plaintext letter is *I*.

Continuing with the same approach, the second cipher letter is *F*. Shifting this by three letters, the corresponding plaintext letter is *C*.

Continuing with the same method through all the cipher letters, you will finally see that the decrypted message reads:

I came, I saw, I conquered!

How rousing! Thank you, Julius Caesar, for the inspiration!

3

CIPHERS, THE NEXT GENERATION

Caesar Cipher: Not Everything It Was Cracked Up to Be

While Julius Caesar may have thought he was pretty clever encrypting secret messages for his army, in reality, the messages weren't all that hard to decode. No doubt, if an enemy were to have intercepted *L fdph, L vdz, L frqtxhuhg!*, initially they'd think the message was nothing more than gibberish. But with a bit of code-breaking smarts, it probably wouldn't take the enemy long to decrypt the message to "I came, I saw, I conquered!"

The problem with the Caesar substitution was, once the enemy understood the idea behind shifting the alphabet, they could easily crack the code by **brute force** even if they didn't know the shift key used. Brute force is what codebreakers call trial and error. A codebreaker uses brute force to decode an encrypted message by trying every possible combination until they find something that makes sense.

For a Caesar shift, once a codebreaker figures out the shift key, the message is easily decoded. The English alphabet has twenty-six letters, so the shift key has to be a number between one and twenty-five. The codebreaker would simply have to try each shift key starting at 1 until the message translates to something readable. With enough patience, it wouldn't take a codebreaker very long to try twenty-five different possible shift keys.

So even though Julius Caesar was onto something with the Caesar shift, this encryption strategy didn't go far enough to keep his secrets safe. As his enemies started to catch on (and Caesar had plenty of enemies), there was a good chance Caesar's communications would fall into the wrong hands. And at times of war, an intercepted message with a weak cipher could mean game over.

Julius Caesar wasn't the only leader to understand the consequences of a weak cipher.

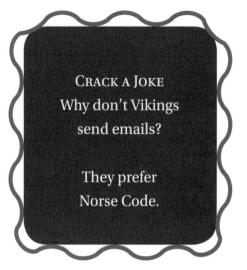

CRACK A JOKE
Why don't Vikings send emails?

They prefer Norse Code.

CRYPTO CHRONICLES

Morse code was invented in the 1830s by Samuel Morse, and it revolutionized long-distance communication. Unlike most codes that are designed to conceal messages, Morse code is a way of *transmitting* messages.

Morse code assigns every letter in the alphabet (along with the numbers zero through nine) a set of dots and dashes. The dots are transmitted across a wire as a short beep, while the dashes are transmitted as a long beep. The operator on the other end of the wire notes the dots and dashes on paper, and is then able to translate the message.

Samuel Morse

Morse code transformed communication, allowing events in one country to be immediately reported in another country. It also changed the nature of warfare, allowing instant communication with troops a long distance away.

One of the most famous uses of Morse code is the universal distress signal: three dots, followed by three dashes, then three dots again (. . . – – – . . .). Since three dots form the letter *S* and three dashes form an *O*, the distress signal came to be known as SOS. Some people mistakenly think SOS stands for "save our ship." The series of dots and dashes that came to be known as SOS was chosen mostly for convenience and technically doesn't stand for anything.

Cousins in Conflict

In the sixteenth century, two cousins, Queen Elizabeth I and Mary, Queen of Scots, were, unfortunately, not the best of friends. Elizabeth was the reigning Queen of England, but she believed Mary was a threat to her throne. Mary had a lot of supporters who did not believe Elizabeth deserved to be queen. These supporters wanted to find a way to replace Queen Elizabeth with Mary. Queen Elizabeth didn't like that very much, so she did what she thought was best to secure her place as queen: she ordered Mary's arrest.

For the next nineteen years, Mary was under house arrest. During this time, she was moved around between different castles. She had servants to take care of her, cook her meals, and clean her rooms. You might think this wasn't such a bad deal for Mary, except Mary was under constant surveillance. She was not permitted any visitors, and every single letter Mary received or sent was intercepted and read by Elizabeth's trusted guards. These guards reported all of Mary's moves back to Elizabeth. As the years passed, and Elizabeth grew more suspicious of her cousin, Mary's living conditions grew worse and worse. Mary was beginning to feel desperate.

Meanwhile, Mary's supporters were growing in number. As if Elizabeth didn't resent her cousin enough! Elizabeth's most loyal advisors urged their queen to eliminate the problem of Mary once and for all. They wanted Elizabeth to order Mary's execution. But Elizabeth wasn't quick to dole out a death sentence. Mary was her cousin, after all. Sentencing family to death wasn't something Elizabeth would do willy-nilly.

Remember all of Mary's supporters? Well, some of them started plotting a secret scheme to kill Queen Elizabeth. With Elizabeth out of the way, Mary could finally step in as the new queen.

Mary's supporters devised a wicked plan to have Queen Elizabeth murdered. They needed to share this plan with Mary, but this was a problem because Mary's every move was being monitored by Elizabeth's guards. The plotters found a way to secretly communicate with Mary. A secret cipher key was developed and smuggled to Mary inside a beer keg. Mary's guards had no idea a secret message had been passed to Mary. With the cipher key delivered, Mary and her supporters could now send encrypted messages back and forth, and since the beer kegs worked so well to hide the cipher, they continued using this delivery method for all their messages. Mary and her supporters had found a way to best the guards.

Or so Mary and her supporters thought.

Eventually, Mary was arrested and put on trial for treason, but even then, Elizabeth was not sure she wanted to sentence Mary to death. This was her cousin! Killing her own blood relative had to have made Elizabeth squeamish. Before ordering Mary's death, she'd need to be absolutely certain of her guilt. She'd need unquestionable proof.

Remember those secret messages smuggled to Mary? Eventually those messages were intercepted by Elizabeth's chief spymaster, a man by the name of Sir Francis Walsingham. But of course, the messages were encrypted so Queen Elizabeth would not be able to understand them, right? If the ciphers were strong enough, there was a chance Mary could escape a death sentence. Mary's life depended on cryptography.

But Mary had put her trust in a weak cipher. Spymaster Walsingham had very smart cryptographers working for him. Those secret messages were a piece of cake to crack.

But that's not all. Walsingham was so devoted to Queen Elizabeth that he wanted to be absolutely certain to eliminate the threat of Mary once and for all. Before turning over the secret messages to Elizabeth he had a postscript added to the end of one of Mary's letters. The postscript was forged in Mary's handwriting and used the same cipher key so it looked like it came from Mary.

According to the new letter, Mary was *authorizing* the assassination of her cousin, Queen Elizabeth. So now, according to the forged postscript, not only did Mary *know* about the planned assassination; she *approved* of the assassination.

Bad news for Mary.

At her trial, Mary was convicted and sentenced to death.

CODING THE CLASSICS

The mystery and secrecy surrounding cryptography and ciphers make for a fascinating story. It's no wonder that cryptography is a popular theme in classic literature.

In Jules Verne's *Journey to the Center of the Earth*, the characters must decrypt a mysterious parchment to begin their journey.

Sir Arthur Conan Doyle also took on the theme of cryptography. In fact, his famous character, Sherlock Holmes, is an expert cryptographer. One of Sherlock Holmes's most impressive cases is told in "The Adventure of the Dancing Men," where the cipher to decrypt consists of dancing stick figures.

Edgar Allan Poe is another classic author who had an interest in cryptography. It is believed that Poe's fascination evolved during his years in the US Army, where cryptography and ciphers are part of military routine. Poe's story "The Gold-Bug" revolves around a cipher that contains information about a buried treasure.

Keys, Words, and Beyond

As codebreakers became better at cracking simple ciphers, like the Caesar substitution cipher, codemakers realized they'd need to do a better job at encrypting secret messages. They invented more advanced encryption processes to try to stop the codebreakers. One such encryption strategy is called the **keyword cipher**. Unlike the Caesar substitution, which uses a shift key, the keyword cipher uses a special *word* as its key.

Here's a hypothetical example. Julius Caesar needs to make sure he can secretly communicate with his army after they leave Rome. Right before his generals march out, he tells them the secret keyword that they will use to decrypt his messages on the battlefield. The keyword in this example is CAESAR, of course, because everyone knows Julius Caesar was pretty self-centered. But how can that word encrypt a message? Here's what he would do.

First, write down all the letters of the alphabet. Next, beneath the alphabet line, write down the keyword, eliminating any letters that appear more than once in the keyword:

A	B	C	D	E	F	G	H	I	J	K	L	M	N	O	P	Q	R	S	T	U	V	W	X	Y	Z
C	A	E	S	R																					

"Caesar" is not misspelled here. The letter *A* already appears in the keyword, so it won't be used again.

Then, fill in the rest of the alphabet in order, but skip the letters that appear in the keyword:

A	B	C	D	E	F	G	H	I	J	K	L	M	N	O	P	Q	R	S	T	U	V	W	X	Y	Z
C	A	E	S	R	B	D	F	G	H	I	J	K	L	M	N	O	P	Q	T	U	V	W	X	Y	Z

With CAESAR as the keyword, all *A*s become *C*s, all *B*s become *A*s, all *C*s become *E*s, and so on. So Caesar's message to his generals would look like this:

Cttcei ct scwl!

When the generals receive the message, they would apply the keyword to translate the cipher:

Attack at dawn!

You can see how with a keyword cipher, the codemakers were getting a little smarter at encrypting messages. Without having the keyword it would be harder—but not impossible—for the enemy to crack a secret message.

Now imagine an encryption strategy where, instead of a simple Caesar key shift or keyword, an additional scrambler is used to mix up the letters even more. How about a strategy that uses two or more keywords in combination? What if the letters in a message are not even replaced with other letters, but rather numbers or symbols? You can see how any of these scenarios would make a codebreaker's job tougher. And that's pretty much the codemakers' number one objective—giving the codebreakers a hard time.

CAMP CRYPTO

Some ciphers substitute letters with other letters (Caesar shift and keyword ciphers are good examples). But there's another type of cipher, called the **Polybius cipher**, that replaces letters with **numbers**.

Here's how it works.

The Polybius square is made of a five-by-five grid. Each square on the grid is filled by a letter. The grid looks like this:

	1	2	3	4	5
1	A	B	C	D	E
2	F	G	H	I/J	K
3	L	M	N	O	P
4	Q	R	S	T	U
5	V	W	X	Y	Z

(Yes, the letters *I* and *J* share a square. They're okay with it. Really.)

To encrypt a message, a letter is replaced by the number from its corresponding row (across) followed by the number from its corresponding column (up and down). For example, to encrypt the letter C, find it on the grid. Then identify the number in its row, followed by the number in its column. So, the letter C would be replaced with the number 13. Encrypting the word "CAT" using the Polybius square would result in the cipher 131144.

Easy, right?

Want to try your hand at codebreaking? How about a riddle?

What goes up but never comes down?

Go ahead and think about it for a few minutes.

Stumped? For the answer you'll need to decrypt this cipher using a Polybius square.

54344542 112215

SYMBOL STUMPER

Oink, Oink

Creating a cipher usually involves exchanging the message's original letters with other letters or numbers so that it appears completely unreadable to anybody who isn't supposed to understand it.

But cryptology is all about hiding secrets, and there are many ways to keep a secret.

Instead of substituting letters with other letters, another strategy someone may use to encrypt a message is to use symbols. One such technique is commonly known as the **pigpen cipher**. It is called the pigpen cipher because the boxes look like pigpens and the dots look like pigs in the pigpens. You're going to have to stretch your imagination a bit to see the pigs and the pigpens, but here is an example of what a pigpen cipher might look like:

□□∟Γ ⟨⊓⟩

Because the cipher uses symbols rather than letters, if someone were to intercept the above message they might not even realize it contained a secret. They might think they were holding random doodles.

In order to decrypt a pigpen cipher, each letter is replaced by a corresponding symbol using the grids below.

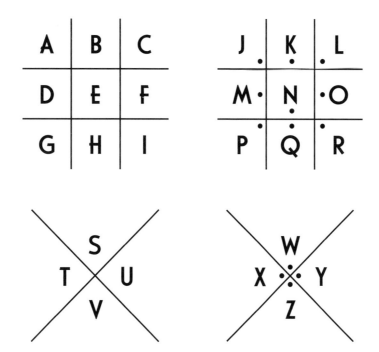

Each letter is represented by the part of the "pigpen" that surrounds it. Take a close look at each letter in the grids above. The lines surrounding each letter, and the dots within those lines, represent the symbol.

So an *A* looks like this: ⌐⌐

B looks like this: ⊔

M looks like this: ⊡

And *Y* looks like this: ⟨

Try to decipher this pigpen message using the pigpen grids.

⌐F⌐L⌐ >∏□ L⌐⊐□

The first letter is represented by the symbol ⌐, which corresponds to the letter *C* in the grid on page 25. Continuing with this method, the second letter is represented by the symbol ⌐, which corresponds to the letter *R*. If you continue decoding the message, you will see that the symbols above translate to:

crack the code

Secret Brotherhood

Many groups used the pigpen cipher for secret communications, but it is perhaps most famously associated with Freemasons, one of history's oldest and most mysterious societies. This is why the pigpen cipher is sometimes referred to as the Freemason's cipher.

Tombstone of James Leeson depicting Freemason symbols

There is much myth and legend surrounding the Freemasons. Many believe the all-seeing eye atop an uncompleted pyramid on the back of the US one-dollar bill is actually a Freemason symbol. It is well known that two of America's earliest presidents, George Washington and James Monroe, were Freemasons. Benjamin Franklin, John Hancock, and Paul Revere are also believed to have been Freemasons.

The Freemasons are known for their secret rituals and customs. There are secret passwords, secret handshakes, and code words. So it's no surprise the Freemasons needed a method to encrypt their messages to keep important matters away from prying eyes. For this, they chose the pigpen cipher. It is believed that the pigpen cipher has been used by the Freemasons since at least the eighteenth century.

One interesting example of the pigpen cipher can be seen today at Trinity Church, located near the business district in New York City. Part of the church includes a cemetery with the tombstone of one James Leeson, who died on September 28, 1794.

Nothing much is known about Mr. Leeson's life, but it seems he has become quite popular in death because of what he chose to decorate his tombstone with: a winged hourglass, a flaming urn, and a compass. All of these images are important Freemason concepts.

But that wasn't all!

Along the top of the tombstone appear a series of square-like markings. Clever codebreakers realized these markings were part of the pigpen cipher, which decodes to: "Remember Death."

Composing a Conundrum

The pigpen cipher is but one example of symbols used to encrypt a message. Can you figure out what the below message says?

Don't be hard on yourself. Neither can the world's best codebreakers!

The above cipher was made by the famous composer Edward Elgar in 1897. You may not know the name Edward Elgar, but if you've ever attended a graduation ceremony, you've probably heard his music. He is the composer of "Pomp and Circumstance," which is the song almost always played at graduations across America.

In addition to being a gifted composer, Edward Elgar had a deep interest in codes and ciphers. One day, Elgar penned the mysterious cipher and sent it to his friend Miss Dora Penny. He had nicknamed his young friend Dorabella, hence the cipher is commonly referred to as the Dorabella cipher.

The Dorabella cipher has stumped codebreakers for over one hundred years. Here's what we do know. The cipher contains eighty-seven symbols; twenty-four of them are unique. These eighty-seven symbols are spread unevenly across three lines. The symbols all appear to be semicircles in different configurations, but if you look very carefully, most of them appear to be the script letter *E* tilted at different angles. Many people speculate this represents Edward Elgar's initials, E. E.

We know little else about the Dorabella cipher and nobody has ever successfully decrypted the message. Many people think that the cipher may not be a message, but possibly musical notes. This is certainly a possibility, considering Elgar was a famous composer. Others disagree and feel strongly the symbols represent a substitution cipher, where one symbol corresponds to one English letter. This too is certainly possible and is exactly what **cryptanalysts** were counting on when they attempted to crack the code. A cryptanalyst is someone who performs an analysis of the cipher and attempts to crack the code by looking for patterns. A "cryptanalyst" is a fancy word for a codebreaker.

A cryptanalyst looking at the Dorabella cipher would try to look for a pattern. Considering there are twenty-four unique symbols in the Dorabella cipher and twenty-six letters in the English alphabet, there's a good chance that each symbol corresponds to an English letter. The Dorabella cipher is fairly short, using only eighty-seven characters, so it's quite reasonable that twenty-four unique letters are used. Most likely, common letters, like *E*, *A*, and *T*, are repeated a few times, while uncommon letters, like *Q*, *X*, and *Z*, may not appear at all. This strategy is called **frequency analysis** and takes advantage of the fact that some letters in the English language appear more frequently than other letters.

And yet, despite using frequency analysis, a very reliable technique that has been used to crack complicated codes, the Dorabella cipher still remains unsolved.

Even the recipient of the message, Dora Penny, was unable to decrypt the message. Julian Lloyd-Webber, the president of the Elgar Society (yes, Edward Elgar has his own historical society) has stated the following about the mysterious composer: "There was also a mischievous side to him. He liked playing tricks on people, and one of those tricks might have been to send that poor girl that thing that was completely undecipherable and he knew it."

So more than a hundred years later, the world's smartest codebreakers may have been victims of one big practical joke by Mr. Edward Elgar!

Twisting Translations

It's important to remember that English letters, or letters in any language, are really just symbols.

Think about that for a moment.

When you see the letter *P*, you instantly know the sound it makes, right?

But the letter *P* is really just a symbol that was assigned that sound when the English language was invented.

Now, let's say you were not an English speaker, but instead a Russian speaker. Some Russian letters have the same sound as their English-looking equivalent, but others have entirely different sounds. If you were a Russian speaker and saw the *P* symbol, the sound that letter makes to you would be entirely different than to an English speaker. That same *P* symbol would now make an English *R* sound. So a Russian would read the word "POT" as "ROT" because the *P* makes a completely different sound in the Russian language.

If you think of foreign alphabets as being symbols, then is it possible to use cryptography to crack a foreign language that you may not understand? You bet it is! If you look at Russian words you might be able to tell yourself: "This is really written in English, but it has been coded with some strange symbols I must now decode." Programs like Google Translate do exactly this—they use cryptography techniques to decode the foreign symbols and translate the words.

This technique was also used by a team of Swedish and American researchers to crack a manuscript now known as the **Copiale cipher**. The manuscript, dated back to the late eighteenth century, contains pages and pages of mysterious symbols and Roman letters. When researchers first looked at the symbols, they weren't sure how to begin decrypting because they didn't even know what language they were decoding to. That's when having a linguist on the team became very handy. A linguist is someone who studies languages. In this case, the linguist had no experience in cryptography but did have experience with machine translation technologies, like Google Translate. Eventually, the team put together enough clues to agree that the original language was probably German. Then the researchers could use known properties of the German language to try to decrypt the manuscript.

It took a while, but eventually their hard work paid off. What they found was a detailed description of a ritual from a secret society called the Oculist Order that apparently had a fascination with eyes and eye surgery.

Creepy? Most definitely. There was even an account of an initiation ritual where the candidate has an "operation" in which a single eyebrow hair is plucked. Totally wacky.

So why was this such an important discovery? Well, besides the fact that cracking an old code is pretty cool, and using the modern science of cryptography to do it is pretty awesome, the decrypted manuscript is important to historians. Secret societies were very popular in the eighteenth century and directly influenced political revolutions. Historians who try to understand how political ideas spread could use the information in this manuscript to help them track the path of political rebellions. You're probably wondering what eye surgery has to do with politics. That part is a little weird, until you realize that the eye is an important symbol used by secret societies. The eye represents seeing, which leads to truth and knowledge.

Can you think of another group that used an eye as their symbol? That's right! The Freemasons' all-seeing eye. See a trend here?

CAMP CRYPTO

Ready for another codebreaking challenge? Try to solve the following riddle using the pigpen cipher.

Everyone has one, but nobody can lose it. What is it?

Answer:

VՈ⌐⌐Ɔ•∀

5

A TALE OF BURIED TREASURES

The Mystery of Thomas J. Beale

Want to find a buried treasure? I bet you do! Who wouldn't?

Maybe all you need to do is crack a mysterious unsolved cipher. Easy, right? One story says there is a huge treasure just waiting to be discovered. And that treasure, today, would be worth more than sixty million dollars.

That's a lot of money, for sure, but the glory of solving a puzzle that has stumped treasure hunters for over one hundred years would also be pretty awesome, wouldn't it?

The legend begins in the town of Lynchburg, Virginia, in the winter of 1820. A mysterious man named Thomas Jefferson Beale checks himself in for an extended stay at the Washington Hotel. The owner of the hotel is a fellow by the name of Robert Morriss.

Thomas Beale spends the next three months at the Washington Hotel, but nobody knows much about him, where he is from, or what brings him to Lynchburg.

After three months, Beale abruptly checks out of the Washington Hotel. He doesn't announce his departure, and nobody knows where he is going. He just up and leaves without a word.

And the town of Lynchburg, Virginia, moves on.

Then, two years later, in the winter of 1822, Thomas Beale returns to the Washington Hotel. He refuses to discuss where he's been for the past two years and still won't talk about his business in Lynchburg. Beale spends the rest of the winter in Lynchburg, going about his business and making steady friends with the locals. But then spring rolls around, and just like two years ago, it's time for Beale to move on. Only this time, he decides to let the hotel owner, Robert Morriss, in on a little secret. Beale has been getting to know Morriss during his stay at the Washington Hotel. He knows Morriss to be a decent and honorable man and trusts him to keep his secret safe.

Beale gives Morriss a locked iron box and tells him the box contains valuable papers. He asks Morriss to keep the box safe until he returns or sends instructions. So Morriss takes the box and puts it in a safe place. He never asks any questions and never tries to pry the box open.

A few months later, Morriss receives a letter from Beale postmarked from St. Louis, Missouri—that's more than seven hundred miles away.

Morriss opens the letter and learns that Beale is traveling the plains hunting buffalo. But the letter also reveals something about the box Beale has left in Morriss's care. In his letter, Beale tells Morriss that the box contains important papers with information about a great fortune. He asks Morriss to be very careful with the box and to guard it for no fewer than ten years. If after those ten years Beale does not return, only then should Morriss crack the lock and open the box.

The letter goes on to explain that the papers within the box would be unreadable without a cipher key, and Beale promises that within the next ten years the key would arrive and the mystery would be explained.

Morriss continued to guard the box for the next ten years as instructed. But Beale never returned to the Washington Hotel. And the promised key? It never arrived, either. Morriss must have assumed Beale and his associates were unexpectedly delayed. After all, these were the 1800s; travel was tricky and complicated at the time. Morriss figured Beale would show up eventually.

Except Beale never did return to Virginia.

And the promised key never arrived.

Morriss was a patient man. He could've opened the box after ten years, but he didn't. After twenty-three years of keeping the box safe, Morriss, admitting Beale was likely never coming back and the key was probably never going to arrive, finally decided to smash open the box.

Inside, Morriss found another letter. This one explained that three years before their first meeting, Beale and some friends set off on a journey across the plains to hunt buffalo. While tracking a herd, they noticed something in the cleft of the rocks that had the appearance of gold. Gold!

The letter went on to say that Beale and his men mined the gold for the next eighteen months. Over the course of eighteen months, they amassed quite the fortune, and a fortune that big had to be protected. The group of men decided to bury all the treasure closer to their families in Virginia, and they entrusted this important job to Thomas Beale. So Thomas Beale checked himself into the Washington Hotel that first time, found a secret hiding place, and buried the treasure. He rode out the winter at the Washington Hotel, then rejoined his buddies in the plains and continued mining gold for the next two years, amassing even more wealth.

What to do with all this additional gold? Bury it with the rest of the treasure, of course. So, back to Lynchburg Beale went for a second time, carrying another batch of treasure to hide away. But on this second trip, he had an additional mission: he needed to find someone he could trust to keep his secret, just in case something happened to him.

The man he selected was the owner of the Washington Hotel, Mr. Robert Morriss.

Besides Beale's letter, there were three additional papers in the box. Each had a string of unintelligible numbers.

These three sheets of paper became known as the **Beale ciphers**.

Three sheets of paper containing three very important, very valuable pieces of information.

71, 194, 38, 1701, 89, 76, 11, 83, 1629, 48, 94, 63, 132, 16, 111, 95, 84, 341, 975,
14, 40, 64, 27, 81, 139, 213, 63, 90, 1120, 8, 15, 3, 126, 2018, 40, 74, 758, 485,
604, 230, 436, 664, 582, 150, 251, 284, 308, 231, 124, 211, 486, 225, 401, 370,
11, 101, 305, 139, 189, 17, 33, 88, 208, 193, 145, 1, 94, 73, 416, 918, 263, 28, 500,
538, 356, 117, 136, 219, 27, 176, 130, 10, 460, 25, 485, 18, 436, 65, 84, 200, 283,
118, 320, 138, 36, 416, 280, 15, 71, 224, 961, 44, 16, 401, 39, 88, 61, 304, 12, 21,
24, 283, 134, 92, 63, 246, 486, 682, 7, 219, 184, 360, 780, 18, 64, 463, 474, 131,
160, 79, 73, 440, 95, 18, 64, 581, 34, 69, 128, 367, 460, 17, 81, 12, 103, 820, 62,
116, 97, 103, 862, 70, 60, 1317, 471, 540, 208, 121, 890, 346, 36, 150, 59, 568,
614, 13, 120, 63, 219, 812, 2160, 1780, 99, 35, 18, 21, 136, 872, 15, 28, 170, 88, 4,
30, 44, 112, 18, 147, 436, 195, 320, 37, 122, 113, 6, 140, 8, 120, 305, 42, 58, 461,
44, 106, 301, 13, 408, 680, 93, 86, 116, 530, 82, 568, 9, 102, 38, 416, 89, 71, 216,
728, 965, 818, 2, 38, 121, 195, 14, 326, 148, 234, 18, 55, 131, 234, 361, 824, 5,
81, 623, 48, 961, 19, 26, 33, 10, 1101, 365, 92, 88, 181, 275, 346, 201, 206, 86,
36, 219, 324, 829, 840, 64, 326, 19, 48, 122, 85, 216, 284, 919, 861, 326, 985,
233, 64, 68, 232, 431, 960, 50, 29, 81, 216, 321, 603, 14, 612, 81, 360, 36, 51, 62,
194, 78, 60, 200, 314, 676, 112, 4, 28, 18, 61, 136, 247, 819, 921, 1060, 464, 895,
10, 6, 66, 119, 38, 41, 49, 602, 423, 962, 302, 294, 875, 78, 14, 23, 111, 109, 62,
31, 501, 823, 216, 280, 34, 24, 150, 1000, 162, 286, 19, 21, 17, 340, 19, 242, 31,
86, 234, 140, 607, 115, 33, 191, 67, 104, 86, 52, 88, 16, 80, 121, 67, 95, 122, 216,
548, 96, 11, 201, 77, 364, 218, 65, 667, 890, 236, 154, 211, 10, 98, 34, 119, 56,
216, 119, 71, 218, 1164, 1496, 1817, 51, 39, 210, 36, 3, 19, 540, 232, 22, 141, 617,
84, 290, 80, 46, 207, 411, 150, 29, 38, 46, 172, 85, 194, 39, 261, 543, 897, 624, 18,
212, 416, 127, 931, 19, 4, 63, 96, 12, 101, 418, 16, 140, 230, 460, 538, 19, 27, 88,
612, 1431, 90, 716, 275, 74, 83, 11, 426, 89, 72, 84, 1300, 1706, 814, 221, 132,
40, 102, 34, 868, 975, 1101, 84, 16, 79, 23, 16, 81, 122, 324, 403, 912, 227, 936,
447, 55, 86, 34, 43, 212, 107, 96, 314, 264, 1065, 323, 428, 601, 203, 124, 95, 216,
814, 2906, 654, 820, 2, 301, 112, 176, 213, 71, 87, 96, 202, 35, 10, 2, 41, 17, 84,
221, 736, 820, 214, 11, 60, 760.

317, 8, 92, 73, 112, 89, 67, 318, 28, 96, 107, 41, 631, 78, 146, 397, 118, 98, 114,
246, 348, 116, 74, 88, 12, 65, 32, 14, 81, 19, 76, 121, 216, 85, 33, 66, 15, 108, 68,
77, 43, 24, 122, 96, 117, 36, 211, 301, 15, 44, 11, 46, 89, 18, 136, 68, 317, 28, 90,
82, 304, 71, 43, 221, 198, 176, 310, 319, 81, 99, 264, 380, 56, 37, 319, 2, 44, 53,
28, 44, 75, 98, 102, 37, 85, 107, 117, 64, 88, 136, 48, 154, 99, 175, 89, 315, 326,
78, 96, 214, 218, 311, 43, 89, 51, 90, 75, 128, 96, 33, 28, 103, 84, 65, 26, 41, 246,
84, 270, 98, 116, 32, 59, 74, 66, 69, 240, 15, 8, 121, 20, 77, 89, 31, 11, 106, 81,
191, 224, 328, 18, 75, 52, 82, 117, 201, 39, 23, 217, 27, 21, 84, 35, 54, 109, 128,
49, 77, 88, 1, 81, 217, 64, 55, 83, 116, 251, 269, 311, 96, 54, 32, 120, 18, 132, 102,
219, 211, 84, 150, 219, 275, 312, 64, 10, 106, 87, 75, 47, 21, 29, 37, 81, 44, 18,
126, 115, 132, 160, 181, 203, 76, 81, 299, 314, 337, 351, 96, 11, 28, 97, 318, 238,
106, 24, 93, 3, 19, 17, 26, 60, 73, 88, 14, 126, 138, 234, 286, 297, 321, 365, 264,
19, 22, 84, 56, 107, 98, 123, 111, 214, 136, 7, 33, 45, 40, 13, 28, 46, 42, 107, 196,
227, 344, 198, 203, 247, 116, 19, 8, 212, 230, 31, 6, 328, 65, 48, 52, 59, 41, 122,
33, 117, 11, 18, 25, 71, 36, 45, 83, 76, 89, 92, 31, 65, 70, 83, 96, 27, 33, 44, 50, 61,
24, 112, 136, 149, 176, 180, 194, 143, 171, 205, 296, 87, 12, 44, 51, 89, 98, 34, 41,
208, 173, 66, 9, 35, 16, 95, 8, 113, 175, 90, 56, 203, 19, 177, 183, 206, 157, 200,
218, 260, 291, 305, 618, 951, 320, 18, 124, 78, 65, 19, 32, 124, 48, 53, 57, 84, 96,
207, 244, 66, 82, 119, 71, 11, 86, 77, 213, 54, 82, 316, 245, 303, 86, 97, 106, 212,
18, 37, 15, 81, 89, 16, 7, 81, 39, 96, 14, 43, 216, 118, 29, 55, 109, 136, 172, 213,
64, 8, 227, 304, 611, 221, 364, 819, 375, 128, 296, 1, 18, 53, 76, 10, 15, 23, 19, 71,
84, 120, 134, 66, 73, 89, 96, 230, 48, 77, 26, 101, 127, 936, 218, 439, 178, 171, 61,
226, 313, 215, 102, 18, 167, 262, 114, 218, 66, 59, 48, 27, 19, 13, 82, 48, 162, 119,
34, 127, 139, 34, 128, 129, 74, 63, 120, 11, 54, 61, 73, 92, 180, 66, 75, 101, 124,
265, 89, 96, 126, 274, 896, 917, 434, 461, 235, 890, 312, 413, 328, 381, 96, 105,
217, 66, 118, 22, 77, 64, 42, 12, 7, 55, 24, 83, 67, 97, 109, 121, 135, 181, 203, 219,
228, 256, 21, 34, 77, 319, 374, 382, 675, 684, 717, 864, 203, 4, 18, 92, 16, 63, 82,
22, 46, 55, 69, 74, 112, 134, 186, 175, 119, 213, 343, 264, 119, 186, 218,
343, 417, 845, 951, 124, 209, 49, 617, 856, 924, 936, 72, 19, 28, 11, 35, 42, 40, 66,
85, 94, 112, 65, 82, 115, 119, 236, 244, 186, 172, 112, 85, 6, 56, 38, 44, 85, 72,
32, 47, 73, 96, 124, 217, 314, 319, 221, 644, 817, 821, 934, 922, 416, 975, 10, 22,
18, 46, 137, 181, 101, 39, 86, 103, 116, 138, 164, 212, 218, 296, 815, 380, 412,
460, 495, 675, 820, 952.

115, 73, 24, 807, 37, 52, 49, 17, 31, 62, 647, 22, 7, 15, 140, 47, 29, 107, 79, 84, 56,
239, 10, 26, 811, 5, 196, 308, 85, 52, 160, 136, 59, 211, 36, 9, 46, 316, 554, 122,
106, 95, 53, 58, 2, 42, 7, 35, 122, 53, 31, 82, 77, 250, 196, 56, 96, 118, 71, 140,
287, 28, 353, 37, 1005, 65, 147, 807, 24, 3, 8, 12, 47, 43, 59, 807, 45, 316, 101, 41,
78, 154, 1005, 122, 138, 191, 16, 77, 49, 102, 57, 72, 34, 73, 85, 35, 371, 59, 196,
81, 92, 191, 106, 273, 60, 394, 620, 270, 220, 106, 388, 287, 63, 3, 191, 122, 43,
234, 400, 106, 290, 314, 47, 48, 81, 96, 26, 115, 92, 158, 191, 110, 77, 85, 197, 46,
10, 113, 140, 353, 48, 120, 106, 2, 607, 61, 420, 811, 29, 125, 14, 20, 37, 105, 28,
248, 16, 159, 7, 35, 19, 301, 125, 110, 486, 287, 98, 117, 511, 62, 51, 220, 37, 113,
140, 807, 138, 540, 8, 44, 287, 388, 117, 18, 79, 344, 34, 20, 59, 511, 548, 107,
603, 220, 7, 66, 154, 41, 20, 50, 6, 575, 122, 154, 248, 110, 61, 52, 33, 30, 5, 38, 8,
14, 84, 57, 540, 217, 115, 71, 29, 84, 63, 43, 131, 29, 138, 47, 73, 239, 540, 52, 53,
79, 118, 51, 44, 63, 196, 12, 239, 112, 3, 49, 79, 353, 105, 56, 371, 557, 211, 515,
125, 360, 133, 143, 101, 15, 284, 540, 252, 14, 205, 140, 344, 26, 811, 138, 115,
48, 73, 34, 205, 316, 607, 63, 220, 7, 52, 150, 44, 52, 16, 40, 37, 158, 807, 37, 121,
12, 95, 10, 15, 35, 12, 131, 62, 115, 102, 807, 49, 53, 135, 138, 30, 31, 62, 67, 41,
85, 63, 10, 106, 807, 138, 8, 113, 20, 32, 33, 37, 353, 287, 140, 47, 85, 50, 37, 49,
47, 64, 6, 7, 71, 33, 4, 43, 47, 63, 1, 27, 600, 208, 230, 15, 191, 246, 85, 94, 511, 2,
270, 20, 39, 7, 33, 44, 22, 40, 7, 10, 3, 811, 106, 44, 486, 230, 353, 211, 200, 31,
10, 38, 140, 297, 61, 603, 320, 302, 666, 287, 2, 44, 33, 32, 511, 548, 10, 6, 250,
557, 246, 53, 37, 52, 83, 47, 320, 38, 33, 807, 7, 44, 30, 31, 250, 10, 15, 35, 106,
160, 113, 31, 102, 406, 230, 540, 320, 33, 8, 48, 107, 50, 811, 7, 2, 113, 73, 16, 125, 11,
110, 67, 102, 807, 33, 59, 81, 158, 38, 43, 581, 138, 19, 85, 400, 38, 43, 77, 14, 27,
8, 47, 138, 63, 140, 44, 35, 22, 177, 106, 250, 314, 217, 2, 10, 7, 1005, 4, 20, 25,
44, 48, 7, 26, 46, 110, 230, 807, 191, 34, 112, 147, 44, 110, 121, 125, 96, 41, 51,
50, 140, 56, 47, 152, 540, 63, 807, 28, 42, 250, 138, 582, 98, 643, 32, 107, 140,
112, 26, 85, 138, 540, 53, 20, 125, 371, 38, 36, 10, 52, 118, 136, 102, 420, 150,
112, 71, 14, 20, 7, 24, 18, 12, 807, 37, 67, 110, 62, 33, 21, 95, 220, 511, 102, 811,
30, 83, 84, 305, 620, 15, 2, 108, 220, 106, 353, 105, 106, 60, 275, 72, 8, 50, 205,
185, 112, 125, 540, 65, 106, 807, 188, 96, 110, 16, 73, 33, 807, 150, 409, 400, 50,
154, 285, 96, 106, 316, 270, 205, 101, 811, 400, 8, 44, 37, 52, 40, 241, 34, 205,
38, 16, 46, 47, 85, 24, 44, 15, 64, 73, 138, 807, 85, 78, 110, 33, 420, 505, 53, 37,
38, 22, 31, 10, 110, 106, 101, 140, 15, 38, 3, 5, 44, 7, 98, 287, 135, 150, 96, 33, 84,
125, 807, 191, 96, 511, 118, 440, 370, 643, 466, 106, 41, 107, 603, 220, 275, 30,
150, 105, 49, 53, 287, 250, 208, 134, 7, 53, 12, 47, 85, 63, 138, 110, 21, 112, 140,
485, 486, 505, 14, 73, 84, 575, 1005, 150, 200, 16, 42, 5, 4, 25, 42, 8, 16, 811,
125, 160, 32, 205, 603, 807, 81, 96, 405, 41, 600, 136, 14, 20, 28, 26, 353, 302,
246, 8, 131, 160, 140, 84, 440, 42, 16, 811, 40, 67, 101, 102, 194, 138, 205, 51,
63, 241, 540, 122, 8, 10, 63, 140, 47, 48, 140, 288.

Morriss learned from the letter that the first sheet of paper revealed the location of the buried treasure, the second described the contents of the treasure, and the third listed all the names of Beale's gold mining friends and provided instructions on how to divvy up the riches among their families.

At this point, you might be asking yourself, why would anyone want to go to such lengths to find buried treasure, only to distribute it to the families of the miners? Wouldn't Morriss want to keep the treasure all to himself? Remember, though, Morriss was a man of honor. He would find the treasure and follow the instructions Beale left for dividing the treasure among the families. And maybe, just maybe, if the families were grateful enough, they'd give him a little reward for all his troubles.

To fulfill Beale's wishes, first Morriss would need to crack the ciphers.

But since the promised key never arrived, Morriss had his work cut out for him.

It's not impossible to crack code without a key; it just takes grit and determination. And Morriss was determined to decode the mysterious ciphers. Still, they continued to stump Morriss for the next twenty years. At the age of eighty-four, Morriss had no choice but to accept defeat. The Beale ciphers had bested him.

Morriss decided to share the Beale ciphers with a friend, in the hope that they would be more successful in carrying out Beale's wishes. We don't know the friend's identity, but it was this person who eventually had a major breakthrough.

And that breakthrough came with the help of the Declaration of Independence.

The Unlocking Book

This clever friend had the idea that the numbers contained in the Beale cipher corresponded to the words in a book or document. This type of a cipher is commonly known as a **book cipher**. A book cipher is a cipher created using a book or document as the key.

If the unnamed friend could find the right source, maybe they could decrypt the cipher.

Let's remember who created these ciphers.

Thomas Jefferson Beale.

And who was the author of the Declaration of Independence?

Thomas Jefferson.

Could this similarity be a simple coincidence? Or could there be a connection?

But there's one more connection that cannot be overlooked. One of the original signers of the Declaration of Independence was one Robert Morris.

No, this Robert Morris is not the same Robert Morriss, owner of the Washington Hotel. Notice the spelling difference between the two names? But the similarity cannot be ignored.

It turned out, the Declaration of Independence was the key to cracking the second Beale cipher.

How was it done?

Let's take a look.

The first number in the second cipher is 115.

To decrypt the cipher, find the 115th word in the Declaration of Independence. This word is "instituted." The first letter of the word "instituted" is *I*, so the first letter of the decrypted message is *I*.

Continuing with this method, the second number in the cipher is 73, and the 73rd word in the Declaration of Independence is "hold." Therefore, the second letter in the decrypted message is *H*.

Following this same process for the entire cipher reveals the following message:

I have deposited in the county of Bedford, about four miles from Buford, in an excavation or vault, six feet below the surface of the ground, the following articles, belonging jointly to the parties whose names are given in number 3 herewith:

The first deposit consisted of one thousand and fourteen pounds of gold, and three thousand eight hundred and twelve pounds of silver, deposited November, 1819. The second was made December, 1821, and consisted of nineteen hundred and seven pounds of gold, and twelve hundred and eighty-eight pounds of silver, also jewels obtained in St. Louis in exchange for silver to save transportation, and valued at $13,000.

The above is securely packed in iron pots, with iron covers. The vault is roughly lined with stone, and the vessels rest on solid stone, and are covered with others. Paper number 1 describes the exact locality of the vault, so that no difficulty will be had in finding it.

Finally, a partial solution! And if the message is to be taken as truth, there is a whole lot of treasure somewhere out there just waiting to be discovered. The decrypted code even confirms that the location of the treasure is described on the first cipher sheet.

Now all that had to be done was to decrypt the first cipher, obtain the location of the treasure, buy a nice sturdy shovel, head to the site, and start digging.

Easy, right?

Not quite.

You might think the Declaration of Independence is the key to cracking the remaining ciphers. Unfortunately, it's not. Using the Declaration of Independence as the key results in a garble of letters, not any real words.

How about a different historical document? The Constitution maybe? Nope, that doesn't work either. The Magna Carta, Articles of Confederation, or Bill of Rights? Nope, nope, and nope.

Frustrated, Morriss's unnamed friend finally decided they would not be able to crack the remaining two ciphers. In 1862, forty-two years after Thomas Beale's first visit to Lynchburg, Virginia, the unnamed friend decided to publish everything they knew about the mysterious ciphers in a pamphlet called *The Beale Papers*. They decided not to reveal their identity because they feared publishing their name on these findings would attract too much unwanted attention. Instead, they entrusted publication to their friend James B. Ward. Today, everything we know about Thomas Beale, the ciphers, and the buried treasure comes from information found within these *Beale Papers*.

THE

BEALE PAPERS,

CONTAINING

AUTHENTIC STATEMENTS

REGARDING THE

TREASURE BURIED

IN

1819 AND 1821,

NEAR

BUFORDS, IN BEDFORD COUNTY, VIRGINIA,

AND

WHICH HAS NEVER BEEN RECOVERED.

PRICE FIFTY CENTS.

LYNCHBURG:
VIRGINIAN BOOK AND JOB PRINT.
1885.

Cover of *The Beale Papers*, published by James B. Ward

A TRAITOR'S CIPHER

Benedict Arnold is known as one of our nation's most notorious traitors because during the American Revolution he decided to change his allegiance and help the British instead of his own country. While a general on the American side, Arnold was awarded command of West Point, a strategic fortification in New York. Arnold's scheme, however, was to surrender the fort to the British.

For Arnold's plan to work, he had to find a way to communicate secretly with his new British friends. His method of choice? Using a book cipher technique.

The Arnold cipher, as it came to be known, was a series of encrypted, secret communications between Benedict Arnold and British Army Major John André. For the secret communication between Arnold and André to work, both men had to possess identical copies of the identical book. The book they used was called *Commentaries on the Laws of England* by William Blackstone.

And so it went. Arnold's messages contained a series of three numbers separated by periods. The first number represented the page number in the book, the second number denoted the line number on that page, and the third number specified the word on that line.

Pretty good plan, right?

For a while, yes. Until American forces captured André carrying papers describing the plot to take over West Point. Too bad André never bothered to encrypt the information on these papers.

With the plot exposed and André arrested, Benedict Arnold knew he didn't stand a chance. So, he ran, narrowly avoiding capture by George Washington's army. Eventually Arnold made it to Britain.

Today, the name Benedict Arnold is synonymous with the word "traitor."

Fortune or Foolery

What we know from the Beale papers is that somewhere out there, there is a lot of treasure just waiting to be found. Or is there?

Could the Beale ciphers and the buried treasure be one elaborate hoax? It's . . . *possible.*

Some people say that the *Beale Papers* were just a scheme carried out by James B. Ward to make a quick buck. They say that James B. Ward created the ciphers as a ploy to get would-be treasure hunters to buy the pamphlet, and that Thomas J. Beale, Robert Morriss, and the unnamed friend never existed. The pamphlet was sold for fifty cents at the time, which is roughly equivalent to thirteen dollars today. If enough people bought it, James B. Ward would rake in a decent income.

To disprove the naysayers, historians have tried to find evidence that Thomas Jefferson Beale did, in fact, exist. They looked at US census records, which show the official government count of the population at a time. A census performed in 1790 does show that several Thomas Beales were born in Virginia, but we don't know if any of them were the *right* Thomas Beale.

But one record found what could be an interesting clue. The St. Louis post office in 1820 has the name Thomas Beall on a customer list. Yes, the name is not spelled the same as the Thomas Beale in question, but it sure is close. And remember that letter Morriss received from Beale in 1822? That letter was postmarked from St. Louis. Could it be that Thomas Beall and Thomas Beale are one and the same, proving the existence of the buried treasure?

Today, nobody can say with certainty whether Thomas Jefferson Beale existed or whether there is still a trove of treasure just waiting to be discovered. What *is* certain is the story has mesmerized treasure hunters for over one hundred and fifty years.

What's more, the legend has had an incredible impact on cryptography and computer research. Because so many cryptographers and computer scientists have tried to develop sophisticated tools to crack the ciphers, we now have advanced cryptography techniques that would never have been possible without the Beale ciphers. Yes, we haven't been successful in cracking the code, but we have made a lot of strides in code cracking strategies. We have Thomas J. Beale to thank for that.

And that's at least something.

Even if it's not an untold amount of wealth and riches.

A book cipher is a great strategy to use when trying to keep a message secret. It's almost impossible for someone to crack a book cipher unless they know which book was used to create the cipher, and given how many millions of books have been written, it's almost impossible to guess which book might be the key. Perhaps this is one of the reasons the Beale cipher has never been cracked.

But what if instead of using a book to create a cipher, an entire book itself is a cipher?

That's precisely what's behind a six-hundred-year-old book known as the Voynich Manuscript. Named after Wilfrid Voynich, the antiques dealer who purchased the strange book, the Voynich Manuscript is

Pages from the Voynich Manuscript

approximately 240 pages and is written completely in unrecognizable glyphs. In addition to these glyphs, which are widely believed to be ciphertext, the book also features bizarre pictures of plants, zodiac symbols, and people in crazy-looking plumbing contraptions.

What's that all about?

Nobody knows!

We can assume that whatever the Voynich Manuscript is describing must have been very important if someone took the time to write 240 pages of ciphertext and create elaborate drawings. There are all kinds of theories about what the Voynich Manuscript might be describing. Some people have said it's an ancient alchemy book that contains the secret to turning other metals into gold. Others have guessed it's the work of a young Leonardo da Vinci, who wrote in code to keep secrets from the Inquisition. Still others have guessed it's the work of aliens who left the book behind after a visit to planet Earth.

If cryptographers can't decode the words, perhaps we can guess the meaning of the book from the pictures—except, the plants drawn cannot be identified even by botanists. The zodiac symbols look sort of like the zodiac symbols we see today, but they don't really tell us much of anything. And the people in weird plumbing contraptions? Yeah, nobody has a clue what that's all about.

Many Voynich scholars think the manuscript is some kind of medical or pharmaceutical guide. Keep in mind, back then astrology and the zodiac were all tied to medicine and health, so it's certainly a reasonable guess.

CAMP CRYPTO

Question: What gets wetter and wetter the more it dries?

Not sure? Here's a cipher of the answer:

61 12 66 89 176

Try decoding the cipher using the Declaration of Independence as a key, just like the second Beale cipher.

To help you out, here is the first part of the Declaration with the words numbered.

.

When(1) in(2) the(3) course(4) of(5) human(6) events(7) it(8) becomes(9) necessary(10) for(11) one(12) people(13) to(14) dissolve(15) the(16) political(17) bands(18) which(19) have(20) connected(21) them(22) with(23) another(24) and(25) to(26) assume(27) among(28) the(29) powers(30) of(31) the(32) earth(33) the(34) separate(35) and(36) equal(37) station(38) to(39) which(40) the(41) laws(42) of(43) nature(44) and(45) of(46) nature's(47) god(48) entitle(49) them(50) a(51) decent(52) respect(53) to(54) the(55) opinions(56) of(57) mankind(58) requires(59) that(60) they(61) should(62) declare(63) the(64) causes(65) which(66) impel(67) them(68) to(69) the(70) separation(71) we(72) hold(73) these(74) truths(75) to(76) be(77) self(78) evident(79) that(80) all(81) men(82) are(83) created(84) equal(85) that(86) they(87) are(88) endowed(89) by(90) their(91) creator(92) with(93) certain(94) unalienable(95) rights(96) that(97) among(98) these(99) are(100) life(101) liberty(102) and(103) the(104) pursuit(105) of(106) happiness(107) that(108) to(109) secure(110) these(111) rights(112) governments(113) are(114) instituted(115) among(116) men(117) deriving(118) their(119) just(120) powers(121) from(122) the(123) consent(124) of(125) the(126) governed(127) that(128) whenever(129) any(130) form(131) of(132) government(133) becomes(134) destructive(135) of(136) these(137) ends(138) it(139) is(140) the(141) right(142) of(143) the(144) people(145) to(146) alter(147) or(148) to(149) abolish(150) it(151) and(152) to(153) institute(154) new(155) government(156) laying(157) its(158) foundation(159) on(160) such(161) principles(162) and(163) organizing(164) its(165) powers(166) in(167) such(168) form(169) as(170) to(171) them(172) shall(173) seem(174) most(175) likely(176) to(177) effect(178) their(179) safety(180) and(181) happiness(182)

THE MAKING OF AN ENIGMA

So you want to send a secret message to your friend, like a real spy? Maybe you've decided to use a substitution cipher, just like Julius Caesar. Great idea. Go ahead and start encrypting your message.

The first thing you'll do is pick a key. Then you'll need to calculate the cipher letters of your message. No big deal. Just shift every letter of your message over by the number in your key.

Except, it can be a bit of a pain if you have a long message.

The previous sentence is fairly short, containing just forty-five letters. And that's just one sentence! If you have several sentences, or maybe even several paragraphs that you're trying to encrypt, you're going to have a lot of letters to deal with. It will probably take you some time and effort to calculate the cipher letters and encrypt a long message.

What does a spy with a lot to say need to do?

That's where a **cipher disk** might come in handy.

The cipher disk was a tool invented in 1470 by Leon Battista Alberti to make encryption and decryption faster. Spies across the universe rejoiced!

The cipher disk was built using two circular plates, and looked like the following figure.

The larger plate, on the outside, was fixed in place, but the smaller plate, in the middle, could spin.

Cipher disk invented by
Leon Battista Alberti

If someone wanted to encrypt a message using this cipher disk, they would first need to pick a key. In the figure above, notice that the letter *A* on the inner ring lines up with the letter *N* on the outer ring. When the cipher disk is set to this position, the key is A = N. It's important to only share this secret key with the intended recipient of the message.

Having set the key on the cipher disk, it would now be ready to encrypt a message. The sender wouldn't need to touch the disk again to encrypt their entire message.

Encrypting the message is now very easy. Let's say the sender needs to encrypt the word "CAB" using the key A = N on the pictured cipher disk. The key has already been set so *A* lines up with *N*. The next step is to map every letter in the plaintext word, "CAB," with a corresponding cipher letter. To do this, find the first letter of the plaintext word, *C*, in the inner ring and note the corresponding letter in the outer ring. In this case, the letter is *L*. Continue with this method and you will see that the plaintext word "CAB" corresponds with the cipher LNM.

There's one catch. In order for the recipient to easily decrypt the message they would need two things: an exact replica of the cipher disk and the key.

The cipher disk, and many variations on the cipher disk, was such a useful way to encrypt messages, it was still being used four hundred years later to send secret messages during the US Civil War.

CRYPTO CHRONICLES

The author of the Declaration of Independence and the third president of the United States, Thomas Jefferson, relied quite heavily on cryptography to keep important messages safe. In fact, Thomas Jefferson was such a cryptography scholar that he invented his own cryptography device called the wheel cipher. The wheel cipher consisted of a series of disks that were spun to scramble the letters of a message. The encryption strategy of the wheel cipher was so strong, it was even being used 150 years later during World War II.

Thomas Jefferson's wheel cipher

There is a lot of historical evidence that proves codes and ciphers were extremely important to Thomas Jefferson throughout his presidency. One notable example is Jefferson's communication with explorers Meriwether Lewis and Lewis Clark during their expedition in the western United States. Jefferson wanted to make sure the discoveries made by Lewis and Clark would never fall into the wrong hands, so he insisted that his communication with the explorers during the expedition be encrypted.

Spinning Secrets

The cipher disk used by the Union Army in the Civil War was invented by Albert J. Myer. Myer is best known for starting the US Army Signal Corps. The Signal Corps was a very important division of the Union Army, responsible for communicating war messages

Myer cipher disk used by the Union Army during the Civil War

across battlefields. The system, invented by Myer, used flags that signalmen waved in different patterns. Each flag-waving pattern was a code! Someone across the battlefield could see the flags being waved and would be able to translate the pattern into a message. But Myer wanted to make communications across the battlefield even more secure. He decided to invent his own version of the cipher disk.

Myer's version of the cipher disk, seen in the picture above, used only the numbers 1 and 8 in different combinations on its outer ring. The inner movable ring had all the letters of the alphabet placed in a random order. In the middle he placed his initials, A.J.M., so everyone would know this was his creation. It was a cool invention. He deserved to brag a little, especially because the cipher disk became such an important part of the Union war effort. In reality, a message encrypted with a cipher disk isn't too hard to crack using brute force. It's really just a tool to make encrypting messages with the substitution cipher a little easier. If a clever codebreaker really wanted to decrypt a message encrypted with a cipher disk, they could probably get it done without breaking too much of a sweat—until 1918, when a German inventor named Arthur Scherbius decided to expand on the basic idea of the cipher disk to create the most fearsome encryption machine the world has ever known. That machine was called **Enigma**.

German Enigma machine used during World War II

It was Enigma that helped shape World War II, the deadliest war in history.

WANTED: CITIZEN ARCHIVISTS

President Abraham Lincoln knew how important secret communication was to winning the Civil War. That's why he often communicated with his army using codes.

As technology evolved during the course of the war, Lincoln began relying on telegrams for communication. Telegrams allowed Lincoln to communicate with his army on the battlefields in real time. A telegram is an old-fashioned messaging system that transmits words across a wire. It's sort of like text messaging today, except not as fast, not as accurate, and not as easy to send and receive. But the idea is similar. Lincoln could type a message, send it across a wire, and the message could be read by the recipient some distance away very quickly.

Lincoln and the Union Army sent thousands of telegrams during the course of the war. But important messages were encrypted to make sure the Confederate Army couldn't intercept them. Just what did those telegrams say? That's been unclear for a very long time.

Over 150 years have passed since the Civil War, and we are only now beginning to decrypt the secret communications.

And you can help!

An organization called Decoding the Civil War is looking for 75,000 citizen archivist volunteers to help decrypt thousands of telegram messages sent during the course of the war. The information gathered from this effort will lead to a better understanding of the events that helped shape our nation.

Think you have what it takes to be a citizen archivist?

To enlist, head over to: www.zooniverse.org/projects/zooniverse /decoding-the-civil-war

Code of Combat

Just what was Enigma, and why was it so dangerous?

On the surface, Enigma looked like an ordinary, old-fashioned typewriter. It doesn't look very fierce, does it? Certainly nothing an army should worry about, right?

But this simple-looking machine gave the Germans a very important leg up during the war, and that's because under the covers, Enigma was so much more than a harmless-looking typewriter.

Enigma, put simply, is a cipher machine. If someone wanted to encrypt a message using Enigma, they would type the message using a standard keyboard, just like you would type using a computer keyboard. Except when you type on a computer keyboard, the letters you type appear on a monitor, right? Well, with Enigma, a different set of letters—the ciphertext—lit up on a lampboard on the Enigma machine. The operator would note the letters illuminated on the lampboard and jot them down on a separate sheet of paper. Now the secret message was encrypted and could be sent to its intended recipient by courier without worry. Even if the message was intercepted by the enemy, the sender could be sure that the enemy would not be able to crack the message and understand its meaning.

In fact, the Germans were positively confident that messages encrypted by Enigma could never be cracked. It was absolutely unbreakable. Enigma was their secret weapon. Enigma would help them with the war.

And for a very long time, they were right.

To understand why Enigma was so

Enigma machine being used by the German military on the battlefield

powerful, we need to take a peek inside. What we discover is that Enigma is a big old cipher disk!

Except, unlike the old-fashioned cipher disks used for hundreds of years, these cipher disks were built using modern technology, electrical engineering, and advanced mathematics. You could say the cipher disk invented by Alberti got a major upgrade!

Let's take a look at how Enigma worked.

The first thing you need to know is that you need one Enigma machine to encrypt a message, and a second, identical Enigma machine to decrypt the message. During World War II, the Germans had many Enigma machines spread out across battlefields.

At the heart of the Enigma machine are three cipher disks that work together to create very strong ciphertext. If one cipher disk could do a good job encrypting a message, you can imagine that three cipher disks, working together, would make the message even tougher to crack. And that's exactly the idea behind Enigma. In fact, later models of the machine went even further, using five cipher disks. The more the better!

The cipher disks used in the Enigma machines were called scramblers.

The scramblers were the magic behind Enigma. Before a message could be encrypted, each of the three scramblers would need to be set to a precise starting position. Remember, two Enigma machines are needed for communication; one to encrypt the message, the other to decrypt the message. As with earlier cipher machines, the encrypting and decrypting machines had to have the exact same starting positions. These positions can be thought of as the key to encrypting and decrypting a message. They were recorded in carefully guarded codebooks that were given only to people encrypting and decrypting Enigma messages. Codebooks were very secretly distributed. The codebooks were so important that sometimes they were printed in soluble ink. If the Germans ever suspected that the enemy was drawing closer, they could put water on the pages and wash away all the information, protecting the valuable codebook information.

How many different possible starting combinations are there for the three scramblers? Each scrambler has twenty-six different starting positions, corresponding to twenty-six letters in the German alphabet. So there are twenty-six ways to configure the first scrambler, twenty-six ways to configure the second scrambler, and twenty-six ways to configure the third scrambler. Altogether, that's

$$26 \times 26 \times 26 = 17{,}576$$

That's a lot of possible starting positions! You can see why just guessing the key was not a very practical option.

What if an eager enemy agent wanted to try all 17,576 possible keys? Well, if they worked night and day, it would probably take them about two weeks to try every combination. By then, the key would have changed—the code changed every day—and they'd have to start all over again. Now, what if *twenty* eager enemy agents all got together, bought a couple of pizzas, and divvied up the job of trying all possible combinations? Well, in that case, they'd probably break the key within a day, which could be very damaging to the German forces.

It's not surprising that the designers of Enigma thought 17,576 possible starting positions just wasn't enough. They needed to give Enigma more starting keys. So they added a feature to allow the scramblers to be mixed around in different configurations. Yes, they scrambled the scramblers. Go figure!

How many different ways are there to arrange three different scramblers? Let's take a look. Below is a representation of three scramblers in an Enigma machine.

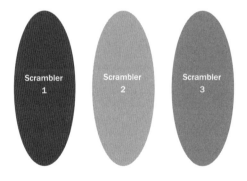

But it's also possible to arrange the scramblers in any of the following sequences:

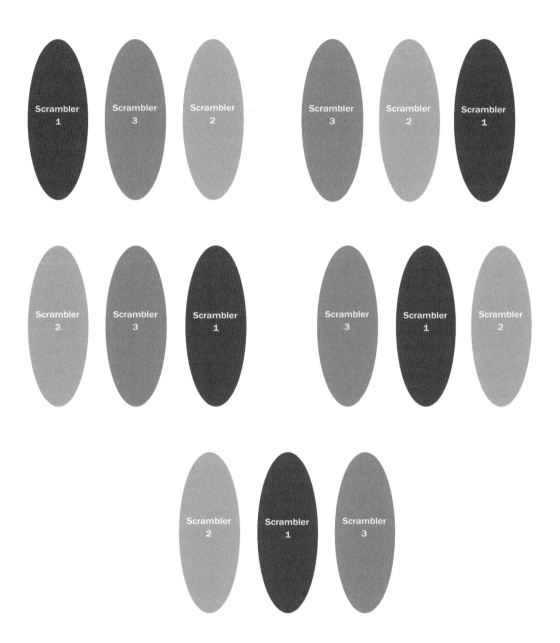

Now you can see there are six different possible ways to arrange the three different scramblers. How does this change the number of possible Enigma keys? We need to do some more math. By allowing the scramblers to be arranged in six different possible positions, the equation to calculate the number of possible starting positions is now:

$$26 \times 26 \times 26 \times 6 = 105{,}456$$

That's a lot of possible keys! It certainly would be very hard to guess the key, but not impossible. So the designers of Enigma had to make cracking Enigma even harder.

Up until now we've been talking only about the starting position of the three scramblers. The magic behind Enigma is a clever little trick: after encrypting every letter, the scramblers *turn*!

Here's how it worked. Every time an operator would press a letter on the keyboard, an electrical signal would travel through the Enigma machine's scramblers. The cipher letter would then be illuminated on the lampboard, and the operator would jot this cipher letter down on a sheet of paper. Inside the Enigma machine, the first scrambler would then turn one notch. So if the operator were to push the exact same letter again, the signal would then travel through the scramblers again but a different letter would be illuminated on the lampboard. In fact, if the operator pushed the same letter over and over again, each time it would be encrypted differently and a different letter would be lit up on the lampboard.

It's easy to see how this would make a codebreaker's job very difficult.

But that was just the first step. The designers of Enigma soon added even more ways to increase the randomness and complexity of the encryption process. After all of the enhancements, there were over 10,000,000,000,000,000 different keys that a single Enigma machine could be configured with. With so many possible combinations, the Germans were confident no communication encrypted with Enigma could be intercepted and decrypted by the enemy. And they were absolutely right. Even when Allied forces were able to get their hands on an Enigma machine, without the codebook there was no way for them to decrypt German messages—unless they were willing to try 10,000,000,000,000,000 keys. Were they willing? You bet they were! Did they try? They sure did. But they couldn't break the messages. They really needed the German codebook that contained the keys. Or did they?

Breaking the Impossible

It was early in the war when an eclectic mix of people gathered at Bletchley Park, Britain's code and cipher school located not far from London, England. The diverse group included mathematicians, cryptographers, chess players, crossword puzzle fans, and many other specialists. The group's goal? Take down the fiercest coding machine the world had ever known. No pressure, right?

The Bletchley Park crew, led by super genius Alan Turing, took advantage of one important flaw in Enigma's otherwise bulletproof system: Enigma must be operated by a human, and humans like habit.

Alan Turing

Alan Turing asked the following questions:

Since Enigma relied on human operators, could human habits find their way into Enigma's coded messages? Could these habits give clues to help crack the code?

Fortunately for Bletchley Park, the answer to these questions was yes.

Let's pretend you're a German agent responsible for distributing a weather report to the front lines. Weather could have a strong impact on military operations. If a storm unexpectedly blows through during a covert operation it could jeopardize the entire mission. Since your job is to send daily weather reports, it's safe to assume your reports will have similar formats every day. For example, you may start your report every day as follows:

To: The Front Lines
Subject: Weather Report

After Enigma encrypted the message, it might look something like this:

BG: FRE LPSDQ MZOJD
QUALPR: AXBQJDF PLANTU

Initially, someone intercepting that message would not be able to tell what it said. But if that same someone knew that you sent a message every day with the weather report, they might be able to pick up some clues to help decipher the message, even if they didn't have the key.

For example, they would probably guess that the word "weather" would appear somewhere in the message, and they probably might even know approximately where the word "weather" would be found in the message.

These types of clues were called **cribs**. Even though the cribs were very small clues, they were enough to get Bletchley Park started. If they knew that AXBQJDF may be the word "weather," then all they had to figure out was which Enigma setting would produce this ciphertext. This meant they had to test all the possible combinations until one of those settings translated WEATHER into AXBQJDF. Easy, right? Wrong. Remember, there are 10,000,000,000,000,000 possible settings.

But one clue is better than no clues.

Alan Turing and the Bletchley Park team began picking apart hundreds of intercepted messages looking for similar cribs. It took a lot of work, but by piecing together many clues, and with the help of lots of engineering, eventually they were able to crack Enigma messages.

By 1945 almost all German Enigma traffic could be decoded within a day or two by the British. The Germans had no idea Enigma had been cracked, so they kept on sending messages via Enigma throughout the war not realizing their enemy was reading their secret communication. This historic achievement finally turned the tide of the war and stopped the German Army. Many people agree that World War II was won not only by soldiers on the battlefield, but also by engineers cracking the code.

Cryptography really can make or break a nation.

The Bombe That Burst the War

In order to decrypt an Enigma encrypted message, engineers at Bletchley Park first had to look for clues in the message. These clues were called cribs. But even with these cribs, it was still too hard to find the key to crack the entire message. With over 10,000,000,000,000,000 possible keys it was too much work to try every possible key by pencil and paper.

To solve the problem, Alan Turing invented a machine called Bombe.

After the cribs were identified, this information was fed into a Bombe. With this information, the Bombe was able to quickly check all remaining key possibilities. The Bombe did this by imitating many Enigma machines running at the same time, trying all possible key options until it found the right one.

Finally, a way to quickly crack Enigma messages without manually trying billions of key possibilities!

Bombe machine used at Bletchley Park

At the end of the war, most Bombes were destroyed because England wanted to keep everything that happened at Bletchley Park top secret. Many years later, when the government decided it was finally okay to start celebrating, a replica of Bombe was built and placed at the Bletchley Park museum.

CODING HEROES: CODE WHISPERERS

The attack on Pearl Harbor by the Japanese finally brought America into World War II.

America realized it needed a way to keep messages private from its Japanese enemy. Of course, during the war, Americans used various encryption techniques, but encrypting a message takes a lot of time and effort. If the American military wanted to quickly transmit instructions, they'd have to find another way.

And for that, they asked for some help from American Indians, especially the Navajo nation.

The Navajo language was not widely understood. In fact, it was believed that only thirty people outside the Navajo nation could understand the language. This made it a perfect secret code.

Navajos—and members of thirty-two other tribes—were enlisted or drafted into the marines and trained as **code talkers**. Their job was to transmit military information over telephone and radio. During the invasion of Iwo Jima, six Navajo code talkers sent more than eight hundred messages. None of these messages were decoded by the enemy. Were it not for the code talkers, the marines never would have taken Iwo Jima.

Following the war, the code talkers continued to treat their work as top secret. For this reason, most people never knew the role American Indians played in winning the war. It wasn't until 2001, when President George W. Bush awarded the Congressional Gold Medal to four surviving original code talkers, that this contribution was first publicly recognized.

CODING HEROES: INVISIBLE CRYPTOLOGISTS

Arlington Hall Junior College for Girls was established as a private women's school in 1927, but it didn't stay a school for very long. In 1942, the US government shut down the school and took possession of the building to use for army operations. A man by the name of William Coffee worked at the school as a waiter, then was hired as a junior janitor for the Army's Signal Intelligence Service (SIS).

William Coffee receives award for his service during the war

In 1944, when SIS was ordered to increase employee diversity, a manager approached Coffee, a black man, to ask for his help. Coffee did such a good job recruiting talented black workers that he was eventually put in charge of the team. By 1945, Coffee managed thirty people. Their jobs? Processing foreign coded messages. In the early part of the war, most of the messages Coffee's team decoded had to do with international business, especially between two of America's biggest wartime enemies, Germany and Japan. The team was responsible for filtering through tons of messages to find anything that might be useful to the war effort.

Because of Jim Crow laws, which forced black workers to be segregated from white workers, Coffee's team did not interact with white workers at Arlington Hall. The group of cryptanalysts worked tirelessly to keep America safe, but they were forbidden from using the same lunchroom, lounges, or bathrooms as their white coworkers. The cryptanalysts working with Coffee were vital to the government, but they were virtually invisible. Most white employees working at Arlington Hall during World War II had no idea a team of black cryptographers existed.

In 1946, William Coffee was awarded the Commendation for Meritorious Civilian Service. He worked in cryptology for the government until his retirement.

CODING HEROES: WOMEN OF THE WAR

A few months before the attack on Pearl Harbor, mysterious letters began appearing in the mailboxes of young women at America's most prestigious female colleges. The letters invited the recipient to an interview.

At the interview, only two questions were asked:

1. Do you like crossword puzzles?
2. Are you engaged to be married?

If the women answered that, yes, they liked crossword puzzles, and, no, they were not engaged to be married, then they were allowed to attend a secret meeting. There, they were given the opportunity to work for the US military as cryptanalysts. If they agreed to continue with the program, they would be trained in codebreaking techniques. There was just one catch. They could not tell anyone about this program. Not even their parents or friends.

It turned out, while young men were overseas on the battlefield, the US military desperately needed educated, smart women to help with the war effort. They recruited women at the top of their class to join the clandestine operation. There were at least ten thousand women codebreakers who served during the war. They decoded messages on enemy strategy, battlefield casualties, pending attacks, and supply needs. All along, the women kept a vow of secrecy. Nobody knew what their job was. Most of their friends and families assumed they were working as secretaries or janitorial staff.

The operation lasted until the end of World War II. After the war, these hardworking women, who had worked in secret, were merged into what is now the National Security Agency, or NSA.

CODING HEROES: CARRIER PIGEONS

In 2012, a homeowner in England was cleaning out his chimney and made an incredible discovery.

In addition to finding lots of twigs, dead leaves, and other gunk, the homeowner found the remains of a pigeon—but this was no ordinary pigeon. This pigeon was a World War II carrier pigeon. Historians believe this brave little bird was on a mission to deliver a message from Allied forces in Nazi-occupied France back to England.

Sadly, the brave little spy pigeon never made it to its destination. It seems it decided to stop to catch its breath for a moment, before continuing on its long journey, but, alas, fell off its perch and tumbled down an open chimney. There, this feathered hero came to rest—with a vital message still strapped to its leg.

Nearly seventy years after the end of World War II, the secret message was finally found, safe and sound, hiding in a red cylinder strapped to the remains of the pigeon.

The problem is, the message was written in cipher, and nobody has been able to figure out what it says. To this day, the pigeon cipher has never been cracked.

The discovered code

Carrier pigeons were important soldiers during the war because they could reach speeds of eighty miles per hour and fly distances of seven hundred miles. That's about what a modern car can drive on two full tanks of gas! The British army trained 250,000 birds in World War II as members of the National Pigeon Service. Once enlisted, and having completed their training, the spy birds would be dropped into enemy territories using mini parachutes. The birds were then picked up and secret messages, sealed in red capsules, were strapped to their legs. The birds would then be released to fly home to deliver the important message. Some pigeons were even outfitted with small cameras so they could take aerial pictures of enemy positions during their journey home.

CAMP CRYPTO

Alice has sent you an encrypted message.

f al klq qorpq bsb. vlr pelria klq qorpq ebo bfqebo. jbbq xq ifyoxov xcqbo pzelli?

You know she encrypted the message using a cipher disk. You previously agreed on the key, so you set the cipher disk to the correct position to decrypt Alice's message. Your cipher key is now set to look like this:

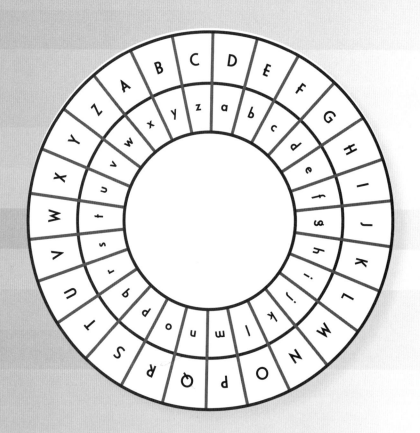

What is Alice's message telling you?
Hint: The outside ring is plaintext, the inner ring is cipher text!

THE MYSTERY OF *KRYPTOS*

Sculpting a Stumper

Ciphers are certainly useful to people like Bob and Alice who want to keep information away from nosy eavesdroppers like Eve. But cryptography is more than just passing notes in class about the latest gossip without anybody finding out. Countries around the world depend on cryptography to keep their citizens safe.

The US government encrypts all top-secret information using the most advanced encryption technology, ensuring nobody can access its most important secrets. These ciphers are not done by pencil and paper. They are so complicated and so advanced that powerful computers must be used. This way the government can be absolutely sure that even if a hacker were somehow able to break through the government's security system they'd probably find cipher text that could not be easily decrypted, even with the most advanced codebreaking technologies.

Perhaps to demonstrate just how seriously our government takes cryptography, one of the most famous unsolved ciphers of all time is sitting in plain sight on the grounds of one of our nation's most important government headquarters: the Central Intelligence Agency (CIA). A good spy organization needs top-notch cryptographers and cryptanalysts to keep our secrets safe and to steal secrets from our enemies. And yet at CIA headquarters in Langley, Virginia, where hundreds of the world's smartest codebreakers go to work every day, none of them have been able to solve the mystery of *Kryptos*.

Who is the mastermind behind this confounding cryptographic mystery? Surely a master codemaker with advanced degrees in mathematics, science, and engineering? Wrong. The creator of *Kryptos* is . . . a gifted artist, specifically, a sculptor named Jim Sanborn. The mystery that has confounded codebreakers for over twenty years is a ten-foot-tall copper sculpture. Located in the courtyard of CIA headquarters, *Kryptos* was installed in 1990. It resembles a scroll and contains exactly 1,735 alphabetic letters.

The word "kryptos" means "hidden" in Greek.

A cipher.

The *Kryptos* cipher is broken down into four parts. The first three parts of *Kryptos* have already been decoded.

But part four of *Kryptos* is still a mystery.

Unraveling the Puzzle

The first three parts of *Kryptos* were cracked by CIA agent David Stein after he spent nearly four hundred hours' worth of lunch breaks trying to solve the puzzle. Stein used only paper and pencil as his tools to crack the code. It took nearly eight years for Stein to solve the first three parts, but the CIA didn't tell anyone when he did. This allowed a computer scientist in California, Jim Gillo-

Kryptos sculpture located at CIA headquarters

gly, to steal the spotlight a year later when he announced that he'd also cracked the same three sections. The only difference? Unlike Stein, Gillogly used a computer.

So how was *Kryptos* solved? The hard part was figuring out the key. For part one, there are actually two keywords needed to solve the cipher. The first keyword is "kryptos." It doesn't take a genius to figure out why Sanborn chose "kryptos" as one of the keywords. The second keyword is "palimpsest." This one isn't as obvious.

Palimpsest? What does that mean?

The dictionary defines "palimpsest" as follows:

noun

a parchment or the like from which writing has been partially or completely erased to make room for another text.

Erasing text and replacing it with new text? This definitely sounds like something a cryptography specialist would be interested in. Notice that *Kryptos* itself resembles an ancient scroll. A palimpsest, perhaps?

THE UNBREAKABLE CODE

As cryptography evolved, codemakers found ways to make encrypted messages harder to crack, but codebreakers continued to find advanced ways to crack them.

Was there any way to keep a secret safe?

Was there an unbreakable code?

For almost three hundred years the answer was yes. The solution to all the codemakers' woes was the **Vigenère cipher** (pronounced vidj-en-air).

When the Vigenère cipher was developed it was hailed as a brilliant, revolutionizing method of cryptography. For a long time it was believed that the Vigenère cipher could never be cracked.

Until it was cracked.

Those codebreakers just don't give up. So it was back to the drawing board for the codemakers.

Even though today there are techniques to crack the Vigenère cipher, it's not that easy. This is likely the reason artist Jim Sanborn decided to use it for **Kryptos**.

Now that you know the two keywords, "kryptos" and "palimpsest," you can easily crack the cipher, right? Well, not quite. That's just one piece of the puzzle. Next, you'd need to take the keywords and run them through a cryptography algorithm called the Vigenère cipher. Want to see the Vigenère cipher in action? Head on over to Camp Crypto at the end of the chapter to see how *Kryptos* part one was solved.

The suspense must be killing you! I know you're dying to know the solution, so let's cut right to the chase. The cipher decrypts to the following:

Between subtle shading and the absence of light lies the nuance of iqlusion.

Huh?

What's that supposed to mean?

You will notice that the word "illusion" is misspelled as "iqlusion." People think this was done on purpose by artist Jim Sanborn, and it might be a key to help crack other parts of *Kryptos*.

We know this sentence was authored by the artist. There are several theories on what this sentence might mean. Many believe it is simply a poetic phrase; others believe it points to hidden messages. Your guess is as good as theirs!

To decrypt section two of *Kryptos*, codebreakers needed to find new keywords to unlock the cipher. It turns out the first keyword used is "kryptos," just like in section one, but the second keyword is "abscissa." What's an abscissa? An abscissa is a mathematical concept involving distance on a plane. Cryptographers love their math!

Breaking the code reveals the following perplexing message:

It was totally invisible. How's that possible? They used the earth's magnetic field. x The information was gathered and transmitted undergruund to an unknown location. x Does Langley know about this? They should: it's buried out there somewhere. x Who knows the exact location? Only WW. This was his last message. x Thirty eight degrees fifty seven minutes six point five seconds north, seventy seven degrees eight minutes forty four seconds west. x Layer two.

Well, that's confusing, isn't it?

The message is obviously designed to sound like a secret agent spy telegram, which would make some sense, given we're dealing with the CIA.

To help understand the message, you can assume the *x*'s are sentence breaks used, just like a period, to mark the end of a sentence. But that helps only a little. You may have noticed the word "underground" is spelled incorrectly as "undergruund." You can assume that Sanborn deliberately misspelled the word. It's likely an important clue, but nobody has figured out why. The message also refers to something "buried out there somewhere." Did Sanborn bury something somewhere on CIA headquarters grounds in Langley? It is definitely a possibility. Sanborn has been asked this very question by many reporters. He's not talking (but he did share some details about his life and hobbies. Check out the sidebar on page 69 for some possible clues).

The decrypted message states that only "WW" knows the exact location. Who is WW? Most people believe the WW referred to in the decoded message is William Webster, the former director of the CIA. Sanborn was asked to provide Webster with the solution to the puzzle. At *Kryptos*'s dedication ceremony, Sanborn handed Webster an envelope, sealed with wax, that supposedly held the solution to the puzzle. The CIA had assured Sanborn they would place the sealed envelope containing the solution in a vault without opening it. Well, Sanborn reasoned if the CIA kept their promise the envelope would stay sealed, so what difference would it make if Sanborn didn't put the actual solution in the envelope? And that's exactly what he did. He tricked the CIA! Sanborn has confirmed that, other than him, nobody has the solution to *Kryptos*.

And what about the coordinates mentioned in the decrypted solution: 38°57'6.5"N 77°8'44"W? The point is about 150 feet southeast of the sculpture itself. Could it mean something is buried on this spot? Nobody knows. Is it possible? Sure! But it's not like any citizen can walk in to the CIA's top secret headquarters with a shovel to dig and see what they might find.

And if someone who works at the CIA *has* tried to dig on this spot, and *has* found something, they're not talking. Remember, the CIA loves their secrets.

The third section of *Kryptos* was decoded using a transposition technique, scrambling the letters until a message revealed itself. The third section was much more complicated to solve than the first two sections, but with some keen crypt-analysis the following message was revealed:

Slowly, desparatly slowly, the remains of passage debris that encumbered the lower part of the doorway was removed. With trembling hands I made a tiny breach in the upper left-hand corner. And then, widening the hole a little, I inserted the candle and peered in. The hot air escaping from the chamber caused the flame to flicker, but presently details of the room within emerged from the mist. x Can you see anything q?

The passage is a description from archaeologist Howard Carter's diary on the day he discovered King Tut's tomb.

Any guesses as to why a description of opening an Egyptian king's tomb is so important? Some people believe it is a metaphor for the wonders of discovery, just like the journey of discovery codebreakers take to crack *Kryptos*. Others think the passage, or possibly Howard Carter's book, may be a key to solving the unsolved section of *Kryptos*. But mostly, people are just guessing.

Did your keen codebreaking eyes notice the word "desperately" spelled incorrectly? Careless error? Likely not. For the record, that's three misspelled words in three *Kryptos* sections. That can't possibly be a coincidence, could it?

SECTION OF *KRYPTOS*	MISSPELLED WORD	CORRECTLY SPELLED WORD
1	iqlusion	illusion
2	undergruund	underground
3	desparatly	desperately

What could these misspelled words be telling us? Could it be Jim Sanborn was careless? Just a bad speller?

Most definitely not.

These are probably important clues to help solve the mystery of *Kryptos*.

As for section four of *Kryptos*, this mystery continues to remain unsolved. Jim

Sanborn confirmed that he designed part four to be, by far, the most complicated piece of the *Kryptos* puzzle to crack. The fact that part four is only ninety-seven characters long makes it much harder to solve, because there are not enough cipher characters to find a pattern. There's most certainly a trick to solve it, but nobody has figured it out yet. Can you? Here's the cipher:

O B K R U O X O G H U L B S O L I F B B W F L R V Q Q P R N G K S S O
W T Q S J Q S S E K Z Z W A T J K L U D I A W I N F B N Y P V T T M Z F P K W
G D K Z X T J C D I G K U H U A U E K C A R

Perhaps because Sanborn had started growing tired of waiting for codebreakers to solve section four, in 2010 he released an important clue hoping to help the codebreakers along a bit. Sanborn announced that the sixty-fourth through sixty-ninth letters in the cipher, corresponding to cipher letters NYPVTT, decrypt to the word "Berlin," as in the capital of Germany.

WHO IS THIS MYSTERY MAN?

Jim Sanborn, the son of two artists, grew up knowing next to nothing about cryptography. He wasn't even a great math student. He needed a tutor throughout high school just to help him pass his math classes. The exception to that was geometry. Not surprisingly, the budding sculptor loved the mathematics behind shapes.

Artist Jim Sanborn

Growing up, Sanborn had an interest in science. He confessed that he even tried building a cyclotron particle accelerator in his basement before wisely realizing it probably wasn't a very safe idea to invest too much time in a nuclear hobby. He redirected his interest in science toward experimenting with electricity. Sanborn's other interests included archaeology and paleontology. Sanborn described finding several large dinosaur skeletons on a dig when he was a teenager and donating them to the Smithsonian Institution. Sanborn decided to get a college degree in sculpting because he wanted to use art to investigate these other interests.

So, how did Jim Sanborn, a man with no background in ciphers or cryptography, build such a confounding cryptographic mystery?

When Sanborn was asked to design a piece of art worthy of CIA headquarters, he decided to incorporate the idea of a puzzle because people identified the CIA with puzzles, intrigue, spies, and secret codes. Since Jim Sanborn knew nothing about cryptography he asked his friend Ed Scheidt for help. Scheidt, a retired CIA cryptographer, knew a thing or two about making ciphers and shared his knowledge with Sanborn.

But not even Ed Scheidt knows the solution to *Kryptos*.

Today, Jim Sanborn makes his home in Washington, D.C. People ask him all the time for the answer to *Kryptos*.

Jim Sanborn isn't talking.

This important clue should have helped things along a bit, right?

It didn't.

After another four years with no progress, Sanborn released another clue. The next five cipher letters, MZFPK, decrypt to the word "clock."

For sure that final clue must have given codebreakers a huge push to solve this puzzle, right?

Nope. It didn't.

Codebreakers have loads of theories as to what Sanborn's *Kryptos* part four clue, Berlin clock, might refer to.

Sanborn has noted in interviews that the collapse of the Berlin Wall in Germany in 1989 was "big news" at the time he was designing *Kryptos*. The Berlin reference, together with the latitude and longitude coordinates decrypted in section three, could be referring to the location of a Berlin Wall monument on the CIA grounds.

And what about the clock? The Berlin Clock, otherwise known as the Set Theory Clock, is a code in and of itself. It displays the time through illuminated colored blocks rather than numbers and requires a complicated calculation to figure out what time it is.

Math again!

So why is part four so hard to crack? Sanborn has said that part four uses a much stronger encryption technique than the rest of *Kryptos*. It's simply a harder cipher to decode. Sanborn has confirmed that a few people have managed to solve the beginning of the message, but their solution falls apart as the message continues. He's also stated that as computers get more powerful, it's probably only a matter of time before someone, ultimately, hits upon the full solution.

If it's not solved, eventually Sanborn will release a new clue. Just how long will he wait before releasing a new clue? He's not sure. Whenever he feels the time is right. Only eighty-six more cipher letters to crack the *Kryptos* code.

CAMP CRYPTO

Ready to solve the mystery of *Kryptos* just like a CIA agent?

Remember, the keywords for part one are "kryptos" and "palimpsest."

Let's examine how to use these words to solve the first part of the sculpture. Remember, it took America's brightest cryptanalysts eight years to figure out how to do this. Here we go!

The cipher text for part one is as follows:

EMUFPHZLRFAXYUSDJKZLDKRN

SHGNFIVJ

YQTQUXQBQVYUVLLTREVJYQT

MKYRDMFD

To begin decrypting the cipher text we rewrite the cipher with the keyword "palimpsest" written above the cipher message over and over again.

```
P A L I M P S E S T P A L I M P S E S T P A L I M P S E S T P A
E M U F P H Z L R F A X Y U S D J K Z L D K R N S H G N F I V J


L I M P S E S T P A L I M P S E S T P A L I M P S E S T P A L
Y Q T Q U X Q B Q V Y U V L L T R E V J Y Q T M K Y R D M F D
```

Next, we need to build what is called a Vigenère square, which is basically a big grid of letters. To build the Vigenère square we use the second keyword, "kryptos."

This is what the Vigenère square looks like

STEP 1:
Look! Here's the keyword KRYPTOS!

K	R	Y	P	T	O	S	A	B	C	D	E	F	G	H	I	J	L	M	N	Q	U	V	W	X	Z
R	Y	P	T	O	S	A	B	C	D	E	F	G	H	I	J	L	M	N	Q	U	V	W	X	Z	K
Y	P	T	O	S	A	B	C	D	E	F	G	H	I	J	L	M	N	Q	U	V	W	X	Z	K	R
P	T	O	S	A	B	C	D	E	F	G	H	I	J	L	M	N	Q	U	V	W	X	Z	K	R	Y
T	O	S	A	B	C	D	E	F	G	H	I	J	L	M	N	Q	U	V	W	X	Z	K	R	Y	P
O	S	A	B	C	D	E	F	G	H	I	J	L	M	N	Q	U	V	W	X	Z	K	R	Y	P	T
S	A	B	C	D	E	F	G	H	I	J	L	M	N	Q	U	V	W	X	Z	K	R	Y	P	T	O
A	B	C	D	E	F	G	H	I	J	L	M	N	Q	U	V	W	X	Z	K	R	Y	P	T	O	S
B	C	D	E	F	G	H	I	J	L	M	N	Q	U	V	W	X	Z	K	R	Y	P	T	O	S	A
C	D	E	F	G	H	I	J	L	M	N	Q	U	V	W	X	Z	K	R	Y	P	T	O	S	A	B
D	E	F	G	H	I	J	L	M	N	Q	U	V	W	X	Z	K	R	Y	P	T	O	S	A	B	C
E	F	G	H	I	J	L	M	N	Q	U	V	W	X	Z	K	R	Y	P	T	O	S	A	B	C	D
F	G	H	I	J	L	M	N	Q	U	V	W	X	Z	K	R	Y	P	T	O	S	A	B	C	D	E
G	H	I	J	L	M	N	Q	U	V	W	X	Z	K	R	Y	P	T	O	S	A	B	C	D	E	F
H	I	J	L	M	N	Q	U	V	W	X	Z	K	R	Y	P	T	O	S	A	B	C	D	E	F	G
I	J	L	M	N	Q	U	V	W	X	Z	K	R	Y	P	T	O	S	A	B	C	D	E	F	G	H
J	L	M	N	Q	U	V	W	X	Z	K	R	Y	P	T	O	S	A	B	C	D	E	F	G	H	I
L	M	N	Q	U	V	W	X	Z	K	R	Y	P	T	O	S	A	B	C	D	E	F	G	H	I	J
M	N	Q	U	V	W	X	Z	K	R	Y	P	T	O	S	A	B	C	D	E	F	G	H	I	J	K
N	Q	U	V	W	X	Z	K	R	Y	P	T	O	S	A	B	C	D	E	F	G	H	I	J	K	L
Q	U	V	W	X	Z	K	R	Y	P	T	O	S	A	B	C	D	E	F	G	H	I	J	K	L	M
U	V	W	X	Z	K	R	Y	P	T	O	S	A	B	C	D	E	F	G	H	I	J	K	L	M	N
V	W	X	Z	K	R	Y	P	T	O	S	A	B	C	D	E	F	G	H	I	J	K	L	M	N	O
W	X	Z	K	R	Y	P	T	O	S	A	B	C	D	E	F	G	H	I	J	K	L	M	N	O	P
X	Z	K	R	Y	P	T	O	S	A	B	C	D	E	F	G	H	I	J	K	L	M	N	O	P	Q
Z	K	R	Y	P	T	O	S	A	B	C	D	E	F	G	H	I	J	K	L	M	N	O	P	Q	R

Now we get to work to crack the cipher.

P A L I M P S E S T P A L I M P S E S T P A L I M P S E S T P A
E M U F P H Z L R F A X Y U S D J K Z L D K R N S H G N F I V J

L I M P S E S T P A L I M P S E S T P A L I M P S E S T P A L
Y Q T Q U X Q B Q V Y U V L L T R E V J Y Q T M K Y R D M F D

The first letter of the keyword "palimpsest" is *P*, and this corresponds with the cipher letter *E*. We need to find the letter *P* at the column on the left, then go across the row to the letter *E*. The row across the top where the letters cross is the decrypted letter. The first letter of the decrypted message is *B*.

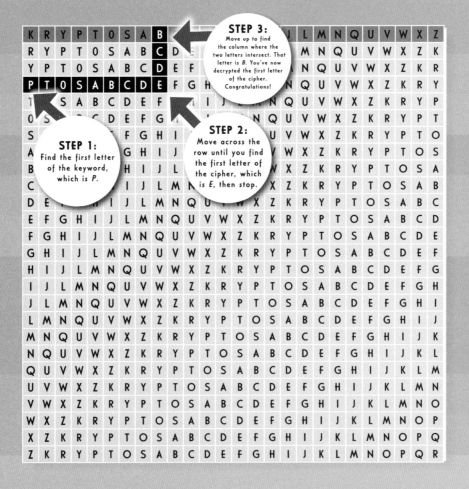

STEP 3:
Move up to find the column where the two letters intersect. That letter is *B*. You've now decrypted the first letter of the cipher. Congratulations!

STEP 1:
Find the first letter of the keyword, which is *P*.

STEP 2:
Move across the row until you find the first letter of the cipher, which is *E*, then stop.

Let's try to decrypt the second letter using the same strategy.

P A L I M P S E S T P A L I M P S E S T P A L I M P S E S T P A
E M U F P H Z L R F A X Y U S D J K Z L D K R N S H G N F I V J

L I M P S E S T P A L I M P S E S T P A L I M P S E S T P A L
Y Q T Q U X Q B Q V Y U V L L T R E V J Y Q T M K Y R D M F D

The second letter of the keyword is *A* and it corresponds with the cipher text letter *M*. We find the letter *A* in the column on the left, then move across until we find the letter *M*. They intersect at the column that starts with the letter *E*.

STEP 1:
Look! Here's the answer!

Continuing with this same technique, you will see that the first part of *Kryptos* decrypts to the following cryptic message:

BETWEEN SUBTLE SHADING AND THE ABSENCE OF LIGHT LIES THE NUANCE OF IQLUSION

8

BEYOND CRACKING THE CODE

Hacking Away at It

The *Kryptos* sculpture at CIA headquarters is more than just a challenge for code-breakers. The fact that one of the US government's most elite agencies, the CIA, is home to one of the world's most mysterious ciphers shows how seriously the government takes **information security**. "Information security" is a term used to describe all the different ways to defend information from unauthorized access. Cryptography is one form of information security, but there are many others. Putting important papers in a safe can be a form of information security. A diary with a lock and key to keep secrets away from your little sister is another form of information security.

Information security is not just important for governments; it's important for everyone. Corporations like banks consider information security to be a top priority. It would be very damaging to their business if information about their customers' account numbers, credit cards, or money balances were to be made public. Medical institutions like hospitals and doctors' offices take information security very seriously because they have a responsibility to keep their patients' medical information private. Universities and schools must consider information security because students' private information like test scores and grades must never be shared publicly.

All of this important information is stored digitally, on thousands of computers and data storage devices. It's important this information stay safe from **hackers.** A hacker is someone who tries (and often succeeds) to gain unauthorized access to a computer system. Hacking a computer system is like trying to pick a lock on a door.

WORD CRACK

The word "hack" first appeared in English around 1200 and meant to "cut with heavy blows in an irregular or random fashion."

Today, the word "hack" is most often understood to mean breaking into a computer system. But it's also commonly used to refer to finding a weird solution to a common problem, like using hair clips to avoid tangling your headphone cords and using rubber bands to keep your shoelaces tied.

Can You Hack The Bank?

Do you think you can hack into a bank's computer system? If you're successful, you might be able to transfer millions of dollars into your personal bank account. Riches galore!

Maybe you can pretend to be the bank president. Sounds like a reasonable plan, doesn't it?

But how do you plan to hack the bank?

Let's assume you figure out how to get to a login screen at the bank. Now what?

You're prompted to enter the bank president's user ID and a password. These are two pieces of information you don't have. What are you going to do now? Guess? Okay, give it a try.

Okay, want to try again? Go for it!

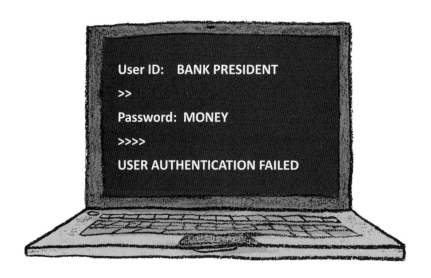

Open Sesame

By now it's pretty clear trying to guess the bank president's user name and password is probably not going to work. You'll be at this for years without success. Even if you figure out the user ID, it's unlikely that you'll be able to guess the password.

That's because most companies have a policy that all employees must use a **strong password**. Insisting on a strong password decreases the chances that someone might guess a password. Passwords are the first line of defense against unauthorized access to a computer. The stronger the password, the more protected the computer will be from hackers.

Guessing a strong password is very difficult and time-consuming, but there may be other ways to get the bank president's password. For example, it's theoretically possible for you to get the bank president's password if you are close enough when they are entering their password and you watch very carefully.

Now you will have access to all the money, right? Wrong.

Sorry! Just having the password might not be enough.

CRACK A JOKE
I needed a password eight characters long . . .
So I picked Snow White and the seven dwarves.

PASSWORD SURVIVAL GUIDE

Yes, it's true. Generating a strong password is annoying. It would be so much easier to make your password "abc123," but that's a bad idea. You don't want someone guessing your weak password.

But at the same time, creating a strong password isn't that easy. If a password is truly strong, with lots of random numbers and symbols, and without real dictionary words, it's probably going to be very hard to remember. If you can't remember your password, what good is it?

Here's a nifty trick to help you remember a strong password.

Make up a sentence you know you can remember that is unique to you. For example:

I go to South Valley School and I'm in the sixth grade!

You can remember that, right?

Now use the first letters of the words in your sentence to generate a strong password:

IgtSVSaIit6g!

Now that's a strong password! It looks like a random string of capital and lowercase letters with a number and symbol tossed in for good measure. Only you know that it relates to a sentence you've selected.

And remember! Never tell anyone your password. It's private!

This is because the bank computer is secured by **second factor authentication.**

Second factor authentication is a security requirement that can be thought of as something you have and something you know. The *something you know* is your password. You've memorized it. Hopefully you're the only person who knows it, but just in case your password has been guessed or stolen, second factor authentication will also require *something you have.*

A common example of something you have might be a cell phone. When you try authenticating to certain systems, as an added level of security you might be sent a text message to your cell phone with a one-time code. To gain access to the system you must have your password (*something you know*) as well as the one-time code delivered to your cell phone (*something you have*). With these two factors, it is very difficult for someone other than you to access the system. Even if someone steals your password, without your cell phone there isn't much a bad guy can do.

The bank president likely has a similar second factor authentication requirement to access important systems. They may carry a **smartcard** as the second factor of authentication. A smartcard looks just like a credit card in size and shape, but inside, there is a small chip that gives an added level of security.

For the bank president to access a very important computer system they would likely need to swipe a smartcard (*something you have*) into a small smartcard reader attached to the computer. They would then enter a password (*something you know*). The computer communicates with the chip inside the smartcard to make sure it's not a fake, and then verifies the entered password. If everything checks out, the bank president is granted access to the computer.

Even if you somehow managed to guess or steal the bank president's password, you probably won't have the smartcard. No chance you're getting through the computer's security system without second factor authentication.

Head, Shoulders, Knees, and Toes

A smartcard is one example of a second factor, but there are many others. **Biometrics** is another form of second factor authentication. Biometrics takes the *something you have* theory a step further to the idea of *something you are.*

Biometrics can use **physical characteristics**, like your face, fingerprints, eyes, or veins, or **behavioral characteristics**, like your voice, handwriting, or typing rhythms, for the second factor of authentication. Using biometrics as the second factor of authentication, rather than a smartcard, has a lot of advantages. Unlike a smartcard, biometric characteristics are impossible to lose or forget. You can't lose your fingerprint or forget to bring it somewhere with you. Biometrics can also be very hard to copy. How would you go about copying someone's eyeball? For this reason, many people consider biometric security to be safer, more convenient, and more powerful. This is real technology happening today, and only one technique to keep

computers safe from bad guys. Iris scanning, like fingerprinting, would be an example of a biometric that relies on physical characteristics—something unique about your body. But some biometric systems rely on *behavioral* characteristics to uniquely identify a person.

Humans like habits. When you put on a pair of pants, do you usually put the right leg on first? Do you avoid stepping on the cracks in sidewalks? Do you like your dinner plate arranged with vegetables on the right and rice on the left? Do you need to have the closet door closed before you go to bed? These are all unique habits that define you. Behavioral biometric systems rely on human habits to uniquely identify a person.

Handwriting is a good example of a behavioral system that could be used to uniquely identify someone. At first glance, using handwriting to identify people might not seem like a good idea. You might think a signature is easy to forge. But good handwriting biometric systems don't just look at how you shape each letter. They analyze the act of writing. They examine the pressure you use and the speed and rhythm with which you write. They also record the sequence in which you form letters, like whether you add dots and crosses as you go or after you finish the word. Unlike the simple shapes of the letters, these traits are very difficult to forge. Even if someone else got a copy of your signature and traced it, the system probably wouldn't accept their forgery.

Biometrics is a growing field that will continue to evolve over the coming years. Cybersecurity professionals like to debate which system is the best; whether it is fingerprinting, iris scanning, handwriting analysis, or countless other possibilities. There are pros and cons for all these biometric options, so it's very hard to say which is the best. What might be the best option for one system may not be the best option for all systems.

One thing is certain, however. A user ID and password is not enough to strongly secure important technology systems. The future will rely on biometric technologies and second factor authentication systems. Eventually, it's not only possible but it's probable that the user ID and password will be entirely eliminated by biometric authentication. That means you won't have to remember all your different passwords. How nice would that be?

FINGERPRINT FLAWS

Fingerprinting has been a very important tool in identifying people. In fact, the US government has more than one million fingerprints on file! But today, most cybersecurity experts agree that fingerprinting isn't a very reliable way to identify someone. That's why, even though fingerprint authentication may be stronger than a plain old password, scientists and engineers are always looking for better ways to prove that someone is who they claim to be.

But isn't it true that a fingerprint is unique and can never change? Doesn't that make it very trustworthy?

Yes, that is true. Your fingerprint can never change and is considered unique. Nobody else shares the same fingerprint as you. Not even identical twins have the same fingerprint.

So why isn't a fingerprint good to use for biometric security? Because a fingerprint can actually disappear.

Some workers, like bricklayers, for example, who use their hands every day, can actually wear down their fingerprints from handling rough materials and heavy equipment all day long. Clerical workers can sometimes wear down the ridges of their fingerprints by handling papers. So think about these problems when you ask yourself what you want to be when you grow up! How much do you value your fingerprints?

EYE AM MORE UNIQUE THAN I THINK

Most people know that fingerprints are unique, which is why they are used to help prove a person's identity. But eye prints are even more unique than fingerprints, and in some ways even more useful. An eye pattern will never change as someone gets older, an eye print can never fade away like a fingerprint might, and it's much tougher to get a booboo on your eye than on your finger.

You may think eye printing is something only for science fiction movies, but that's not true. Eye printing is real and is being used today for biometric second factor authentication.

The most common kind of eye printing is the iris scan. Iris scans use the unique characteristics of the iris—the colored part of the eye—to prove someone's identity. There are approximately 240 unique points in everyone's iris. This is approximately five times more to compare than with a fingerprinting system! You probably never realized just how unique your eyes were!

What makes an iris so unique? Everybody's iris develops a random pattern before they're even born. In fact, the chance of two irides (yes, this is the plural of the word "iris"—go figure?) being identical is estimated to be one in a quinvigintillion. For the record, that is a crazy huge number—a one with seventy-eight zeroes after it! Even identical twins won't have the same iris patterns. And keep in mind, most people have not one but two irides, which, together, make your eyes an even stronger authentication system.

And in case you're worried that an iris scanner will fry your eyes with laser beams—you have nothing to worry about. Iris scanners use light to take photographs of your eyes. The light used is no stronger than the light you'd be exposed to outside on a sunny day.

PRIME TIME

Math Checkup

Today, cryptography is not performed with pen and paper, but rather with powerful computers. The encryption is extremely strong. It is so strong that not only can the encryption never be broken by brute force, but it can't even be broken by extremely powerful computers running day and night for months. This is a very good thing, especially because so much business and communication is handled digitally these days. Without strong encryption, we wouldn't be able to buy things on the internet, listen to music online, watch silly videos on YouTube, or even send emails without worrying that our private information will fall into the wrong hands.

None of this security would be possible without the help of a special category of numbers: prime numbers.

You've learned about prime numbers in school, right? Of course you have! But I bet you never realized prime numbers are the backbone of the modern cryptography universe!

5 divided by **1** = **5**

5 divided by **2** = **2.5** Remainder!

5 divided by **3** = **1.67** Remainder!

5 divided by **4** = **1.25** Remainder!

5 divided by **5** = **1**

5 is a prime number because it can only be divided by itself (**5**) and the number **1**

As a reminder, if a number is prime, it means that the only whole numbers it can be divided by are itself and 1. For example, 5 is a prime number. No two whole numbers can be multiplied together to get the answer 5 other than 5 and 1.

Another way to say this is the only **factors** of 5 are 5 and 1. It's not really hard to check if a small number, like 5, is prime. All you need to do is divide it by all of the whole numbers that come before it. If you have a remainder left over each time, then your original number is prime.

With me so far?

Good.

It's easy to prove whether a small number is prime or not. But, as you can see, it gets harder and takes a lot more computing to test for bigger prime numbers. Below is proof that 17 is a prime number, but notice how many additional calculations are needed—and 17 really isn't *that* big a number.

17 divided by 1 = 17

17 divided by 2 = 8.5 Remainder!

17 divided by 3 = 5.67 Remainder!

17 divided by 4 = 4.25 Remainder!

17 divided by 5 = 3.4 Remainder!

17 divided by 6 = 2.83 Remainder!

17 divided by 7 = 2.43 Remainder!

17 divided by 8 = 2.13 Remainder!

17 divided by 9 = 1.89 Remainder!

17 divided by 10 = 1.7 Remainder!

17 divided by 11 = 1.55 Remainder!

17 divided by 12 = 1.42 Remainder!

17 divided by 13 = 1.31 Remainder!

17 divided by 14 = 1.21 Remainder!

17 divided by 15 = 1.13 Remainder!

17 divided by 16 = 1.06 Remainder!

17 divided by 17 = 1

Seventeen is a prime number because it can only be divided by itself (17) and the number 1—but *boy did that take a lot of work!*

You can imagine that as prime numbers get bigger and bigger, the computing power needed to prove the prime number gets larger and larger. But you'll soon see that very large prime numbers are extremely valuable for cryptography. The bigger the better.

To demonstrate, we need to pick two prime numbers—how about 11 and 19 (don't believe me that these are prime numbers? Go ahead and prove it for yourself!). Now take these two prime numbers and multiply them together.

$$11 \times 19 = ?$$

(Not sure? It's okay to use a calculator.)

Got the answer?

$$11 \times 19 = 209$$

The product of 11 and 19 is 209.

So that was pretty easy.

Now, what if you have no idea what the two original numbers are. All you have is the product, 209, and you have to figure out which two numbers multiply together to make this number.

$$? \times ? = 209$$

Not so easy anymore. It will probably take you a very long time to figure out the factors of 209.

It turns out if you have the product, it's actually really hard to figure out what the prime number factors are. And the bigger the prime numbers you used in your original multiplication, the harder it would be to reverse the math. Let's take another look.

What if I told you that 178,667 is the product of two prime numbers? Can you tell me what those two prime numbers are?

$$? \times ? = 178{,}667$$

Not without a whole lot of work. It might take you hours to find the answer. Maybe even days!

It turns out the two prime numbers multiplied together are:

$$373 \times 479 = 178{,}667$$

It would probably take you about four seconds to do that math equation on a calculator.

It's exactly the same with computers. Calculating 373×479 is superfast on a computer. But asking a computer to find the prime number factors for 178,667 will take the computer some time.

PRIME BREAKTHROUGH

In January 2016, the mathematics world had a landmark discovery: a new prime number!

This new number was discovered with the help of a university computer that ran nonstop for thirty-one days to confirm that the number was, indeed, only divisible by the number 1 and itself.

This prime number, the largest prime number in recorded history, is made up of 22,338,618 digits. This is nearly 5 million digits longer than the previous record. If we were to print this prime number, we would need more than 5,000 sheets of paper!

This special prime number was identified by a University of Missouri professor. As a reward, the professor was given $3,000 in prize money.

Public, Private, and Protected

By now you're asking, just what does all this math have to do with cryptography? I'm so glad you asked!

We'll need Bob and Alice to help explain.

Alice wants to send a private message to Bob across the internet, but she's worried Eve may be listening on the line. That nosy Eve just won't give up!

Alice sends Bob a very strong key that he can use to encrypt messages for her. She makes this key by multiplying two prime numbers together. Here's an example:

$$373 \times 479 = \textbf{178,667} \leftarrow \textit{Here's the key Alice makes.}$$

This key that Alice sends to Bob is called the **public key**. Alice doesn't care if Eve intercepts this public key. It's public! Anyone can have it.

Bob uses this public key to encrypt a message for Alice. You can think of it like this: Bob writes a message for Alice and puts it in a box. Then he uses the public key Alice gave him (in our example, 178,667) to lock the box.

Now that the message is encrypted safe and sound in the box using Alice's public key, Bob sends the message to Alice.

Oh no! That sneaky Eve is snooping on the wire. What if she snatches the message?

There's really nothing to worry about because only Alice has the key to unlock the message. That key is called the **private key**. Alice keeps this private key very safe. The private key is made from the original two prime numbers Alice multiplied together to make the public key.

What two prime numbers multiplied together make 178,667? Only Alice knows they are 373 and 479!

Eve doesn't have Alice's two prime numbers, the private key, so even if Eve manages to get her hands on the locked box, she couldn't open it.

This system of public and private keys is called **public key infrastructure** or **PKI** for short. PKI is the most common encryption system used today to communicate across the internet. The public and private keys used with PKI are not actual keys, but instead very large numbers stored by computers. And the prime numbers used to generate these keys aren't as small as the prime numbers Alice uses in our example. They are enormous prime numbers with thousands and thousands of digits. Each prime number used in a PKI system is so long, it wouldn't fit on one whole page of this book—even in a teeny-tiny font!

The bigger the prime number used, the more secure the encryption. That's why mathematicians and cryptographers are always on the hunt for bigger and bigger prime numbers. You might be surprised to know that prime numbers are still being discovered, but it's true. Since numbers can go on to infinity, there are an infinite amount of prime numbers. We will never know all the prime numbers. The biggest ones are just waiting to be discovered!

When a new prime number is found, we can use that number in cryptography systems to make the encryption much harder to crack. The newly uncovered prime numbers are getting larger and larger, which means that the cryptography systems are getting stronger and stronger. This is bad news for the hackers.

PRIME LAW BREAKER

Everyone who is stealing or trespassing is doing something illegal. If you do something illegal you are breaking the law, and you could be sent to jail.

But most people don't know that it's illegal to have a certain huge number. You read that right. An illegal number. If you have this number, you could be arrested and sent to jail.

What is this illegal number? I already told you, just *talking* about the number could get you in big trouble. It's best not to even *think* about this number.

But you're most likely wondering *why* a number is illegal. That we can talk about.

Not that long ago, if you wanted to watch a movie you'd need to buy or rent a DVD. You couldn't just stream a movie off Netflix whenever you felt like it. You had to physically have a DVD disc that you'd play with a DVD player.

Well, the movie companies really wanted you to buy these DVDs. That's how they made their money, after all. But hackers found a way to copy DVDs by cracking the encryption on the DVD's software. They did this by discovering the prime number that was used to encrypt the digital protection on the DVD.

If hackers could copy DVDs, they could make copies for all their friends or even sell copies to make money. This is called **piracy**. Piracy is the illegal copying or distribution of copyrighted media, and it can get you in a lot of trouble. The movie companies went to court, and a law was passed making it illegal to be in possession of this magic prime number that unlocked DVD encryption.

10

THE WEAKEST LINK

A Cordial Con Job

Even with all the security used to keep information safe, hacks happen every day. Sometimes these hackers know very little about computer systems and how to crack them. Instead, they rely on the computer system's weakest link: the human operator. How does a hacker get past a human sitting behind a keyboard to gain access to information they're not allowed to see? Usually, all they have to do is ask.

Spending months trying to crack a cipher or break into a biometrically locked laptop is too much of a headache for the typical hacker. Most hackers want to get the job done as quickly and easily as possible without getting caught, so they try to find the easiest path into a computer system. In today's digital world, the easiest path into a computer has nothing to do with the computer, and everything to do with being a persuasive person.

Social engineering is the most common method used to hack into a system today. Social engineering relies on the hacker tricking their target into giving them access to a computer.

Imagine a bank robber wants to enter a bank to steal money. If this bank robber looks like a burglar, wearing black clothes, a mask, and a hat that reads THIEF,

there's a good chance they'll get noticed by the bank security guard. The security guard will probably stop them from entering the bank and quickly call the police.

Now, what if that same burglar approached the bank dressed like a businessperson in a fancy suit carrying a serious-looking briefcase? The security guard would probably hold the door open for the robber, wish them a good morning, and allow them to step inside.

The robber just social engineered their way through the front door of the bank. The first step in the plan to rob the bank has worked.

Of course, social engineering a hack on confidential information is a much more complicated procedure, but the same ideas apply. The hacker's goal is to trick a target to gain their trust.

A Testy Trick

Eve has been frustrated ever since Alice and Bob started encrypting messages and making ciphers that are hard to crack. She could continue trying to crack the code and decrypt Alice and Bob's ciphers, but she'll likely never be successful because, through some very good spying, Eve has discovered that the key to decrypt Alice and Bob's ciphers changes every day.

Eve knows she has virtually no chance of decrypting a secret cipher without knowing today's key, so social engineering the unsuspecting friends is her only hope.

Eve walks over to Alice after first period to enact her plan. "You knew about the math test, right? Mrs. Carol told us last week to make sure we study for it."

"Oh . . . um . . . sure. Right. The math test." Alice gathers her books and slams her locker shut. "I have to run, Eve. I'll see you later."

Alice scurries off in the direction of the library.

Of course there is no math test. Eve just played a trick on Alice to distract her. Eve knew that distracting Alice would make her forget to slip today's cipher key into Bob's locker.

Eve is now ready for phase two of her plan. She pulls out a sheet of paper on which she has written the following:

Caesar Shift +1

She slips the paper into Bob's locker. Now Bob has what he believes to be the new key of the day from Alice. He has no idea the key came from Eve and not his best friend. Why would he suspect otherwise? Bob and Alice have just been social engineered by Eve.

Later, Eve manages to snatch a message encrypted by Bob for Alice. Of course, Bob assumes he is using a secret key known only to him and Alice. But Alice is probably still in the library studying for a math test that won't even happen!

Here's the message Eve snatches:

Xbudi pvu gps Fwf! Tif jt vq up tpnfuijoh!

Can you decrypt this code using the key supplied by Eve?

Eve, of course, is quickly able to decrypt the message with the key that she has supplied.

Don't be hard on yourselves, Alice and Bob! Most people would have fallen for this scam. In fact, social engineering is the most popular way hackers are able to penetrate security systems.

Feeling a Bit Under the Weather

One of the most common ways hackers use social engineering to gain access to a computer is through email systems. Here's an example: An employee at a government office receives an email that reads:

Attached is a great picture of you!

What would *you* do if you received such an email? You'd open it, of course. It's a great picture, after all!

Except clicking on the attachment actually runs a program on your computer. The program may infect your computer with **malware**. Malware is short for **mal**icious soft**ware**, and is designed to damage computer systems or steal information from computer systems. One form of malware you may have heard of is a computer **virus.** Just like when you get sick from a virus, when a computer "catches" a virus it gets "sick." And the virus could spread from one computer to another computer. In humans, a virus takes over our immune system and makes us feel lousy. In computers, a virus can take over the system and do unexpected things. Sometimes a computer virus is nothing more than annoying. It might put emojis on your screen or make your keyboard stop working. Other times a virus can be very destructive. Some viruses can steal all the personal information you have on your computer and send it to hackers. Hackers can use this personal information against you.

Viruses are bad news, but computers catch viruses every day. Sometimes the social engineering attacks are so clever, even the smartest cybersecurity professional would fall for it!

In 2015, social engineering was used to hack into the White House. The source? A silly video that showed chimpanzees running around, tormenting human employees. The hacker sent an email from what appeared to be a trusted government email address with the chimpanzee video included as an attachment. When the attachment was opened, the recipient received much more than an entertaining video. Buried within the attachment file was a type of malware called a **Trojan horse.** A Trojan is a harmless-looking computer program that performs dangerous operations, like stealing your passwords or other private information.

Once the hackers cracked open the front door to the White House's system, they were able to use more sophisticated hacking techniques to penetrate even further, all along hiding from government cybersecurity professionals. It took a few months before anybody realized the hackers were inside! The good news? Because all of the most important information stored on White House computers is encrypted, the hackers likely didn't understand all that much. Cryptography for the win!

ANCIENT GREEKS: SOCIALLY AWKWARD?

One of the best examples of a successful social engineering attack comes all the way from ancient Greece, in the city of Troy, during the mythological Trojan War.

As the story goes, Troy was protected by a very high wall that, try as they might, the Greek army was unable to penetrate. Behind their wall, Trojan warriors enjoyed safety as they rained arrows down on the Greek army below.

After fighting, and losing, at Troy for fourteen years, the Greek general, Odysseus, finally had an idea. He ordered his army to pretend to pack up their things and sail away in defeat. As a gift, the Greek army left an enormous wooden horse at the wall. The gift seemed to say to the Trojan army, "We lose. You win. Here's your prize."

The Trojans, celebrating their victory, wheeled the enormous wooden horse through the gates. Little did they know that hidden inside the horse was a small army of Greek soldiers. When night came, the Greek soldiers crept out of their hiding spot, opened the city gates, and let in the rest of the Greek army, which had quietly returned.

The Trojans were swiftly defeated.

Inspired by the tale of the Trojan defeat, a "Trojan horse" has come to mean a trick that causes the enemy to be invited into a secure place. Malware that tricks users into willingly running it is often referred to as a Trojan horse.

S STANDS FOR . . .

When you're on the internet typing in a web address, it almost always begins with http://.

Ever wonder what HTTP means? It stands for hypertext transfer protocol. HTTP is a way for one computer to exchange information with another computer.

Sometimes a web address begins with https://.

What does that extra *S* mean?

The *S* stands for "secure." When you visit a webpage that begins with https:// you know that this website uses hypertext transfer protocol **secure** rather than the basic HTTP. This is an added level of security. Usually websites that require you to enter personal information use HTTPS.

HTTPS ensures that the information you enter on your computer, like your name, birthdate, or credit card information, leaves your computer encrypted. This way, if a hacker were "spying" on the line trying to capture the packet of information before it gets to its destination, they would not be able to understand the cipher. Only the intended recipient is able to decrypt your personal data.

A good example of this would be online shopping sites. When you buy stuff on the internet, you need to provide a bunch of information like your name, address, and credit card number. You wouldn't want this information going to some stranger, right? Do you really want a random stranger knowing that you've just ordered underwear online (even if it was on sale!)? More importantly, you wouldn't want anyone to snatch your credit card information, right? So the online store does everything possible to keep all your personal information (even your underwear size) safe, and that means using HTTPS.

CAN YOU CRACK THE CODE?

11

IT'S NOT AS SIMPLE AS BLACK AND WHITE

Gray Area

Hackers today get a bum rap. They probably deserve it. After all, their mission is to break into computer systems to steal information, right?

Actually, that's not always the case. Not all hackers are bad guys. Some hackers are actually the good guys.

It's true! There's a group of hackers known as **white hats** who are good and decent people just doing their jobs.

White hats are sometimes referred to as **ethical hackers**. Their job is to hack into computer systems and figure out possible holes—holes that can be used to hack into the system. Once they've discovered these holes, they share this information with the computer owners so that all these holes a bad guy might use for hacking can be plugged up. The bad guy hackers are often referred to as **black hats**.

Because technology evolves so quickly, white-hat hackers stay very busy. Just like the battle between codemakers and codebreakers, the war between white hats and black hats is constantly being fought, especially as new applications and programs are being developed at such a rapid pace. As the black hats get better at hacking into systems, the white hats must stay a step ahead, coaching companies like Google, Microsoft, and Twitter, and yes, the US government, on ways to do business more securely in this digital age. There's no slowing down technology, so white-hat hackers have to stay on top of their game.

The term "white hat" comes from old Western movies, where the good guy wore a white cowboy hat. The bad guy always wore the black cowboy hat.

White-hat hackers are so important, some of our nation's biggest companies want to encourage them to keep doing their important work. In 2010, Google started their Security Rewards Program to encourage white-hat hackers to find and report security holes that a black-hat hacker could use to gain unauthorized access to a system. In return, Google provides the white hatters with cash rewards.

Google announced that, in 2014, they paid more than $1.5 million to more than two hundred different white-hat hackers as part of this program.

That's a lot of holes to plug! Just imagine how much safer the digital world is as a result of these cyber warriors finding and reporting all these flaws.

But the most notable result of Google's 2014 Security Rewards Program was this: out of two hundred security flaws reported, the most serious flaw was discovered by a seventeen-year-old kid named George Hotz. As his reward, Hotz earned the largest reward payout of the year, a sum of $150,000. A short while later, Google hired the teenager as an intern in Google's Project Zero division, an elite team of full-time white-hat hackers.

Not a bad job to put on a résumé!

Interested in being a white-hat hacker? You're not alone. And guess what! You don't have to be a grown-up to be an ethical hacker.

At DEF CON, one of the world's largest hacking conventions, held every year in Las Vegas, Nevada, there are special conference sessions held just for kids. At DEF CON Kids, sponsored by r00tz Asylum, kids learn how to be tinkerers, expert codebreakers, and white-hat hackers.

The goal? Teach the next generation of hackers to be awesome. Here's what they have to say: "Hacking gives you super-human powers. You can travel time and space. It is your responsibility to use these powers for good and only good."

Interested in learning more? Check out r00tz.org.

Shut the Backdoor

It's not a good idea to hack into someone else's computer system to steal information or spread malware.

But what if the government wants to hack into *your* system? How would you feel about that?

If you can't hack without getting in trouble, should the government be able to hack you?

Let's ask Alice and Bob.

Alice and Bob have been encrypting their messages to make sure nosy Eve can't understand them. To encrypt these messages, Alice and Bob use an encryption key that is known only to them. Eve,

try as she might, cannot guess the key. She tries hacking their system to break the key, but she is unsuccessful.

Too bad for Eve.

Now imagine that Alice and Bob's teacher, Mrs. Carol, notices Alice passing a secret encrypted message to Bob in the middle of class. She snatches up the message, but when she goes to read the message, it is undecipherable. Of course she can't read it! It's encrypted with a secret key.

Mrs. Carol wants to know what the message says. What if Alice and Bob are planning something sinister to disrupt her class?

She is the teacher, after all. Doesn't she deserve to know what Alice and Bob are plotting?

On the other hand, don't Alice and Bob deserve their privacy?

Tough questions, indeed.

This is exactly the question security experts have been debating for years. Does everyone have a right to encryption? Even the bad guys? And if the bad guys can encrypt their messages, wouldn't it be convenient for law enforcement to have a way to easily decrypt the messages so they can stop a crime from happening? To do that, they'll need the key, but to get the key they'll need to hack into the system, and that could take a very long time and might not even be possible.

Wouldn't it be cool if law enforcement had a magic key that cracked everything that was encrypted? Wouldn't it be awesome if Mrs. Carol had a key to decrypt all of her students' encrypted notes?

In the technology world, this magic key is called a **backdoor**.

To help explain the idea behind a backdoor, imagine a town where everyone has a unique key to their front door. Your key, of course, can't open your neighbor's front door. Your key can only open your front door. But this town is a little different from your typical neighborhood. Here, the police have a master key that can open every back door to every house. If, for whatever reason, the police have reason to suspect that you're up to no good, they can bypass your front door and enter your house from the back with their master key.

That's precisely how a backdoor would work in the technology world—if backdoors actually existed. You see, even though law enforcement agencies, like the FBI, have been asking for backdoors for a long time to help bypass a system's built-in security, technology companies really don't want to provide these backdoors. There are a few reasons for this. For one, most of these technology companies value their customer's privacy. They argue everyone has a right to their privacy and law enforcement shouldn't be allowed to bypass the front door and enter someone's system. Fair enough, but do even bad guys deserve their privacy? Well, in America they do. You've heard the expression innocent until proven guilty, right? It's one of America's most sacred rules of criminal justice.

But there's another reason technology companies hate the idea of a backdoor. If a police officer has a magic key to the back door of every house in the neighborhood, how can someone guarantee that a criminal can't steal that key? Now they'll have easy access to every house in the town.

It's not that technology companies don't want to help the police. It's just that the majority of them believe if they build these backdoors into their systems, there is no way to guarantee that a criminal won't use that backdoor to hack into that system. When we last saw Alice and Bob, their teacher, Mrs. Carol, had intercepted an encrypted note Alice passed to Bob in the middle of class. Mrs. Carol wants to read the message. She fears Alice and Bob are up to no good. Kids these days! Except, just because some kids in the class have been bad in the past (that one time the kids put a whoopee cushion on her chair was not pleasant at all) doesn't mean Alice and Bob are plotting anything sinister. They just don't want Eve reading their secrets. That's all. They have nothing against Mrs. Carol, even though she does assign way too much homework.

But Mrs. Carol is one tough teacher, and she insists on having a master key to unlock all encrypted messages, of Alice, Bob, and everyone else in the class.

How can Mrs. Carol guarantee that this master key won't be snatched by that snooping Eve?

She can't.

And that's precisely why backdoors are problematic.

As convenient as a backdoor would be to law enforcement, for now, at least, it's not happening.

12

CRACKING THE CODE

If you pay attention to the news, it seems like new hacks are happening all the time. The hackers are getting smarter. They are able to crack even the most complicated codes and security protocols.

Are we doomed?

Is any computer safe?

But in fact, technology and the cyber universe are growing, not shrinking. Devices you would not immediately think of, like televisions, air conditioners, washing machines, automobiles, and refrigerators, are now communicating through the internet. Basically, anything with an on/off switch may soon be able to connect to the internet and be controlled by computers. This giant network of connected "things" is known as the **internet of things**, or IoT for short. There is nothing stopping the IoT from growing and growing.

But with the growth of the internet, it's important for cybersecurity professionals to stay one step ahead of the hackers. It's up to the elite cybersecurity warriors, the codemakers, software developers, engineers, and cryptographers, to keep the digital world secure. Yes, technology is changing the way we live, but it's also bringing new challenges. With advanced technology comes the need for advanced cryptography techniques to keep information private and advanced cybersecurity to keep the hackers away.

But what's really the point of all these codes and ciphers? Cybersecurity sure is a lot of work! Why even bother?

Because secrets are important.

Cybersecurity has one mission: protect secrets.

A secret is only a secret if it *stays* a secret. The moment the secret is revealed it is no longer a secret. It is information. Information that was never intended to be released.

Can you crack the code?

Maybe you can. One thing is for certain: knowing how to crack the code is important. But with this knowledge comes great power, and with great power comes great responsibility. It's up to the future codebreakers of the world to use that power for good and keep our cyber universe safe. So carry on! A computer is an amazing tool that opens a door to a wealth of information. Or you can watch silly cat videos all day long. Whatever you choose to do on the computer, have fun, and be smart.

And now, let's put your knowledge to the test. This book is more than just a book. This book unlocks a secret mystery, but only to those codebreakers who have the skills and the smarts to solve the riddle.

Can you crack the code?

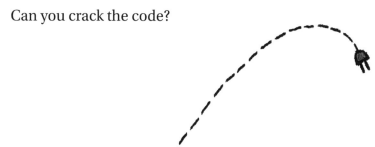

A Final Code

Prove you're a master codebreaker by solving one final cipher.

40.2.1 64.3.5 94.5.3 96.5.2
4.6.3 57.2.13 71.10.4 81.10.5 103.9.3 96.3.3 17.1.13
18.5.1 40.8.4 48.4.4
50.4.1 50.1.4 64.1.4 67.5.3 96.7.4 102.14.12
102.1.3 105.6.4 68.3.1 57.5.2 55.1.5
46.4.9 40.11.4 27.5.12
102.2.6 88.1.1 67.5.9. 56.1.12
53.1.3
38.3.13 38.7.7 6.1.1 51.5.6 58.1.3 66.3.8
81.2.5 38.5.2 29.3.1 28.5.2
46.1.1 25.3.5 54.2.5
65.1.12 77.3.3 81.1.2 2.8.16 11.18.2
17.4.6 28.3.10 30.3.8
51.5.8 65.4.5 36.2.2
103.2.3 2.8.1

Clue: Benedict Arnold was a clever man, even if he was a traitor. Would he have liked this book? Maybe. The *key* is to learn from *this* book.

If you figure out the solution, let me know. Send an email to ISolvedIt@EllasBooks.com.

Barbier, Laetitia. "Morbid Monday: Deciphering an Ominous Cryptogram on a Manhattan Tomb." Atlas Obscura, July 29, 2013. http://www.atlasobscura.com /articles/morbid-monday-the-tomb-of-james-leeson.

Blakemore, Erin. "You Can Help Decode Thousands of Top Secret Civil War Telegrams." Smithsonian.com, June 28, 2016. http://www.smithsonianmag .com/smart-news/you-can-help-decode-thousands-top-secret-civil-war -telegrams-180959561/?no-ist.

Day, Michael. "The Voynich Manuscript: Will We Ever Be Able to Read This Book?" *The Telegraph*, May 24, 2011. http://www.telegraph.co.uk/news/science /science-news/8532458/The-Voynich-Manuscript-will-we-ever-be-able-to -read-this-book.html.

D'Onfro, Jillian. "Google Paid White Hat Hackers More Than $1.5 Million Last Year to Find Bugs." Business Insider, January 30, 2015. http://www.businessinsider.com /google-paid-white-hat-hackers-more-than-15-million-dollars-2015-1.

Durkin, Kevin. "Decoding the Civil War." Verso, June 21, 2016. http://huntington blogs.org/2016/06/decoding-the-civil-war/.

Giles, Jim. "Cameras Know You by Your Walk." *New Scientist*, September 19, 2012. https://www.newscientist.com/article/mg21528835-600-cameras-know-you -by-your-walk/.

Greenberg, Andy. "Meet 'Project Zero,' Google's Secret Team of Bug-Hunting Hackers." *Wired*, July 15, 2014. http://www.wired.com/2014/07/google-project-zero/.

Harmon, Katherine. "Can You Lose Your Fingerprints?" *Scientific American*, May 29, 2009. http://www.scientificamerican.com/article/lose-your-fingerprints/.

Jacobson, Rebecca. "8 Things You Didn't Know About Alan Turing." *PBS Newshour*, November 28, 2014. http://www.pbs.org/newshour/updates/8-things-didnt-know-alan-turing/.

Jevec, Adam. "Semper Fidelis, Code Talkers." *Prologue Magazine* 33, no. 4 (Winter 2001). http://www.archives.gov/publications/prologue/2001/winter/navajo-code-talkers.html.

Jones, Terry L. "The Codes of War." *New York Times,* March 14, 2013. http://opinionator.blogs.nytimes.com/2013/03/14/the-codes-of-war/.

Lee, Joel. "5 of the World's Most Famous and Most Influential White Hat Hackers." MakeUseOf, July 13, 2012. http://www.makeuseof.com/tag/5-worlds-famous-influential-white-hat-hackers/.

MacNamara, Mark. "The Artist of the Unbreakable Code: Composer Edward Elgar Still Has Cryptographers Playing His Tune." *Nautilus*, October 17, 2013. http://nautil.us/issue/6/secret-codes/the-artist-of-the-unbreakable-code.

Markoff, John. "How Revolutionary Tools Cracked a 1700s Code." *New York Times*, October 24, 2011. http://www.nytimes.com/2011/10/25/science/25code.html?_r=3.

Menegus, Bryan. "It's Illegal to Possess or Distribute This Huge Number." Gizmodo, May 3, 2016. http://gizmodo.com/its-illegal-to-possess-or-distribute-this-huge-number-1774473790.

Morgan, David. "9 Things You Didn't Know About Freemasonry." *CBS News*, December 8, 2013. http://www.cbsnews.com/news/9-things-you-didnt-know-about-freemasonry.

Mundy, Liza. *Code Girls: The Untold Story of the American Women Code Breakers of World War II*. New York: Hachette Books, 2017.

Mundy, Liza. "The Secret History of the Female Code Breakers Who Helped Defeat the Nazis." *Politico Magazine*, October 10, 2017. https://www.politico.com/magazine/story/2017/10/10/the-secret-history-of-the-women-code-breakers-who-helped-defeat-the-nazis-215694.

Robinson, Joshua. "NFL's Worst Sin: Losing a Playbook." *Wall Street Journal*, August 24, 2012. http://www.wsj.com/articles/SB100008723963904443584045776098621933055518.

Robson, Steve. "Government's Top Code-Breakers Left Stumped by Wartime Carrier Pigeon's Secret Note Appeal For Public's Help To Decipher Message." *Daily Mail*, November 23, 2012. http://www.dailymail.co.uk/news/article-2237394/Skeleton-hero-World-War-II-carrier-pigeon-chimney-secret-coded-message-attached-leg.html.

Schmeh, Klaus. "The Voynich Manuscript: The Book Nobody Can Read." *Skeptical Inquirer* 35, no. 1 (January/February 2011). http://www.csicop.org/si/show/the_voynich_manuscript_the_book_nobody_can_read.

Schwartz, John. "Clues to Stubborn Secret in C.I.A.'s Backyard." *New York Times*. November, 20, 2010. http://www.nytimes.com/2010/11/21/us/21code.html.

Shachtman, Noah. "They Cracked This 250-Year-Old Code, and Found a Secret Society Inside." *Wired*, November 16, 2012. http://www.wired.com/2012/11/ff-the-manuscript/.

Singh, Simon. *The Code Book: How to Make It, Break It, Hack It, Crack It*. New York: Delacorte Press, 2001.

Singh, Simon. *The Code Book: The Science of Secrecy from Ancient Egypt to Quantum Cryptography*. New York: Anchor Books, 2000.

Sternstein, Aliya. "Common Malware Jimmied Open White House and Anthem Systems, Say Researchers." Nextgov.com, August 13, 2015. http://www.nextgov.com/cybersecurity/2015/08/common-malware-jimmied-open-white-house-and-anthem-systems-say-researchers/119085/?oref=ng-HPtopstory.

Sutherland, Denise, and Mark Koltko-Rivera. *Cracking Codes and Cryptograms for Dummies*. Hoboken, NJ: Wiley, 2010.

Turing, John Ferrier. "Alan Turing's Brother: He Should Be Alive Today." The Daily Beast, June 23, 2012. https://www.thedailybeast.com/alan-turings-brother-he-should-be-alive-today.

Waxman, Olivia B. "A New Largest Known Prime Number Was Discovered." *Time*, January 20, 2016. http://time.com/4187491/new-prime-number/.

Williams, Jeannette, and Yolande Dickerson. *The Invisible Cryptologist: African-Americans, World War II to 1956*. Ft. George G. Meade, MD: National Security Agency, Center for Cryptologic History, 2001.

Wilson, William R. "Codemakers: History of the Navajo Code Talkers." *American History*, February, 1997. http://www.historynet.com/world-war-ii-navajo-code-talkers.htm.

Yagoda, Ben. "A Short History of 'Hack.'" *New Yorker*, March 6, 2014. http://www.newyorker.com/tech/elements/a-short-history-of-hack.

Zetter, Kim. "Finally, a New Clue to Solve the CIA's Mysterious *Kryptos* Sculpture." *Wired*, November 20, 2014. http://www.wired.com/2014/11/second-kryptos-clue/.

Zetter, Kim. "Hacker Lexicon: What Is a Backdoor?" *Wired*, December 11, 2014. http://www.wired.com/2014/12/hacker-lexicon-backdoor/.

Zetter, Kim. "Questions for *Kryptos'* Creator." *Wired*, January 20, 2005. http://archive.wired.com/techbiz/media/news/2005/01/66333?currentPage=all.

They say writing a book is a solitary activity. That's a lie! There are so many people who helped make this book a reality and I am forever grateful.

A huge thank-you to my agent, Clelia Gore, and the team at Martin Literary Management. Clelia has been my champion since that rainy day in New York when we agreed to meet over coffee to talk about all my crazy book ideas. I'm so glad my husband convinced me to meet with you. That day I scored not only the best agent in the universe but a dear friend.

Thank you to the Bloomsbury team for believing in this book series. A super huge thank-you to my editor, Susan Dobinick. Your mentoring and support while writing this book made it sparkle and shine. Lily Williams, you somehow managed to create the cover this book was always meant to have but I was never brave enough to imagine. Cat Onder, thank you for believing in me.

I am indebted to Jim Sanborn who agreed to speak with me about *Kryptos*. When I reached out to Jim to request an interview for this book, I promised I would not ask for any *Kryptos* clues. I stood by that promise. I never asked for any clues . . . directly. I knew interviewing Jim was a massive responsibility, with legions of hopeful code crackers dissecting all his words looking for scraps of hints to help solve the mystery of *Kryptos*. Perhaps observant codebreakers will glean an idea or two from the information shared in chapter seven. If any reader just happens to solve *Kryptos* after reading this book, you're welcome.

Thank you to Secretary Michael Chertoff for meeting with me and providing insight into how the United States government deals with evolving cybersecurity challenges. There are very few people in government circles who understand the challenges facing our nation's systems as well as Secretary Chertoff. In his role as the secretary of the Department of Homeland Security shortly after the September 11, 2001, attacks, Secretary Chertoff shaped what the department would become. I am deeply grateful for his perspective and comforted in his belief that the government is taking cybersecurity seriously.

To my Kidliterati and #MGBetaReader family: there is no better team of writers on the internet. I am forever grateful that we are on this writing journey together. This book would not have been possible without Paul Adams, Becky Appelby, Ronni Arno, Jo Marie Bankston, Rhonda Battenfelder, Brooks Benjamin, Jeff Chen, Melanie Conklin, Abby Cooper, Dana Edwards, Jessica Fleck, Karen Lee Hallam, Colton Hibbs, Laurie Litwin, Jen Malone, Gail Nall, Chris Brandon Whitaker, and vodka wine. Special thanks to #Swapperz Jean Giardina and Brian Sargent. You make me a better writer. Huge love to Jennifer Gracen for being the best pompom-waving cheerleader. Thank you to my very first beta reader, Melinda Cordell.

To my colleagues at Entrust and Cygnacom, you gave me the foot in the door to become a cybersecurity warrior. I have enjoyed a twenty-year career that has been enriching, challenging, and inspiring. Chapter nine is dedicated to you. I think Elmer would have been proud. Special thanks to Peter Bello and Isadore Schoen for their support and mentoring.

My family. You are the reason for everything. To my parents, immigrants to this country who scraped together every penny to provide their daughter with an education. It was unusual for a young girl way back then to be able to pursue an interest in math and science, but my parents sacrificed every day to make sure I had the best education possible. For my boys, Harrison, Sammy, and Nate—the books I write are for you. They are the stories I want you to read and the lessons I want you to learn. You are the inspiration behind these words. Always ask questions. I'll try to find you the answers.

And to Jeff, this crazy writing journey would not have been possible without you. You, quite literally, kept me going throughout the writing of this book. You knew exactly when I needed a jolt of caffeine or a fresh-baked cookie hot from the oven to preserve my sanity. You took over the house so I could have the time I needed to make my deadlines. And when my confidence wavered you provided me with the encouragement, support, and love to reinforce my spirits. This book is for you.

INDEX